Contents

DEDICATION

"Running on Rainbows" is dedicated to my two daughters, Leanne and Kerry, whose aesthetic tastes range from Miro paintings to carburettors, respectively, and to my mother Tib Pope, who taught me water-colour washes for 'proper pictures' at the age of nine, from which age I was considered an "artist" by my peers. Acknowledgements go to Marnie Ives, classroom teacher extraordinaire, who showed me that any five-year-old can do water-colour washes if shown, and who shared many delights and traumas of the "ordinary" classroom; to Harold Armstrong, Coll Wilson, Pat Kratzke and especially Yvonne Handran, Principals, whose recognition of the value of Art education at early ages, enabled much of my research; to Shelley Münster, teacher-aide, who devoted endless hours to the cause of Art for children; to Spina and Mark Ross for their much needed advice; to Martine Zajacek, for long-suffering perserverence with the mammoth task of hand-lettering the text; and to Tim Foley, whose support saved me from starvation, and whose benevolent patronage exceeded that of any Medici.

This second edition is dedicated to my grandson, Josstin, who is yet to make his first magic marks on the living room walls, and to the most important group of people in society, the world over — the educators of our young children.

Second Edition 1993
Publisher: Running on Rainbows Pty Ltd
   P.O. Box 265 Fortitude Valley
   Queensland, Australia 4006
   Telephone (07) 252 2982
   Fax (07) 252 5632
   International enquiries: Telephone 61 7 252 2982

Calligrapher: Martine Zajacek
Illustrations and cover design: Wendy Allen
Life. Be in it. characters: Alex Stitt
Art works: children from Wynnum North, Carbrook and
   Camp Hill Infants State Schools, Queensland,
   Australia, unless otherwise stated
Photography: Wendy Allen, unless otherwise stated
Administrative assistants: Jodie Duthie and Sandy Rodgers
Printer: Harding Colour
   P.O. Box 426
   Cannon Hill
   Queensland, Australia 4170
Typesetting: Harding Colour
   Smartype

First Edition 1989
Publisher: Life. Be in it./Wendy Allen
Printer: Watson Ferguson & Company, Brisbane
Typesetting: S&M Typesetting, Brisbane
Editor: Jarvis Finger
Sponsors: Irene and Jim Cobb of Chroma Acrylics (NSW) Pty Ltd.

ISBN 0 7316 6543 0 (set number)
ISBN 0 7316 6553 8

Line

Line

Let us move with the world around us ~ with the lines of living things and other things that haven't an ounce of life and yet can slide or swivel or bounce or chase. Let us sail hard with a sea-wind, ooze with the coiling of a tree-snake, drift like a log on a silent sea. Give us whirling, swaying, swooping ~ the excitement of rockets lifting slowly from the ground, the dizziness of heights that whizzes round inside us ~ and nights that move to the bump of drums. And if we have to sleep, let us sleep in a swirl of music and the joy of being so much alive.

Contents

SUGGESTED WORK PLAN FOR A BLOCK UNIT OF 10 WEEKS ON LINE

Mix 'n' match your own activities if not following the plan below. Be flexible!
Omit or extend activities where desired or practical. See N.B. p.5, opposite.

WEEK ONE

AWARENESS:	Feeling line	–	ACTIVITY 1...pp.8-10. Vocabulary brainstorming
	Seeing line	–	ACTIVITY 2...pp.11-13. Seeing safari
	Integration	–	ACTIVITY 7...p.27. Drama

WEEK TWO

AWARENESS:	Seeing line	–	ACTIVITY 5...pp.22-23. Line Display
	Integration	–	ACTIVITY 8...p.28. Dance
PRACTICAL:	Experimental "play"	–	ACTIVITY 14...pp.42-44. Painting
	Directed experience	–	ACTIVITY 15...pp.45-46. Painting

WEEK THREE

AWARENESS:	Seeing line	–	ACTIVITY 3...pp.14-15. Audio-visuals · Display
	Integration	–	ACTIVITY 11...p.36. Poems, snippets
PRACTICAL:	Directed experience	–	ACTIVITY 16...p.47. Wall chart discussion
	Applied experience	–	ACTIVITY 17...p.48. Painting

WEEK FOUR

AWARENESS:	Seeing line	–	ACTIVITY 6...pp.24-26. Recording from life
	Integration	–	ACTIVITY 8...p.29. Video. Select one activity
PRACTICAL:	Other media	–	ACTIVITY 19...pp.50-51. Drawing from life

WEEK FIVE

AWARENESS:	Seeing line	–	ACTIVITY 3...pp.16-17. Select an activity/ies
	Integration	–	ACTIVITY 11...pp.36-37. Writing stories, scripts
PRACTICAL:	Other media	–	ACTIVITY 20...p.52. Environmental weaving and/or
			ACTIVITY 22...p.52. Wool collage

WEEK SIX

AWARENESS:	Seeing line	–	ACTIVITY 4...pp.18-21. Appreciation. [Use
			Student's Book also]
PRACTICAL:	Other media	–	ACTIVITY 30·31...pp.56-59. Linear designs

WEEK SEVEN

<u>AWARENESS</u>:	Seeing line	— ACTIVITY 4...pp.18-21. Appreciation cont.
		[Use Student's Book also]
<u>PRACTICAL</u>:	Other media	— ACTIVITY 24·25·26...p.53.Printing. Groups.

WEEK EIGHT

<u>AWARENESS</u>:	Integration	— ACTIVITY 9...pp.31·32. Listening to Music
		ACTIVITY 8...p.30. Painting to Music
<u>PRACTICAL</u>:	Other media	— ACTIVITY 21·23...p.52.Construction, Wire sculpture

WEEK NINE

<u>AWARENESS</u>:	Integration	— ACTIVITY 10...pp.33-35. Line with instruments
<u>PRACTICAL</u>:	Other media	— ACTIVITY 27·28...p.54. Sgraffito, Monoprint

WEEK TEN

<u>AWARENESS</u>:	Integration	— ACTIVITY 12...p.38. Computer graphics
	Language of line	— ACTIVITY 13...pp.39·40. Word display
<u>PRACTICAL</u>:	Other media	— ACTIVITY 18...p.49. Charcoal
		ACTIVITY 29...p.55. Frottage
		ACTIVITY 32...p.60."Doing your own thing" time

N.B. The above Work Plan is a sample of how the program can be used. The most important aspect is that **AWARENESS EXPERIENCES** are done in conjunction with **PRACTICAL EXPERIENCES**, even if there is a time lapse between them, so that students have a source for their own ideas. So mix and match as you wish, as is opportune, as is realistic. Flexibility is the keyword. The plan above covers a wide range of activities ~ if you miss some out in your own plan, try to catch them next year. If you use them all this year, try the extra ones, or your own variations, next year. But remember that **VOCABULARY** is the medium through which we are teaching aesthetic awareness, and that **DRAWING FROM LIFE** is essential for learning to "see".

Also, the practice of several minutes of <u>DAILY DRAWING</u> is highly recommended and highly rewarding ~ as a class or individual activity at the end of work completed in other subjects, in quiet sessions, or "calming down" moments of the day. See also, p.69 of this Unit, COLOUR, p.7, and TONE, pp. 42, 44.

Materials

THE BASIC KIT   — double if possible

CHROMACRYL PAINT — all five colours* ... pp. 30·42-46·48·53·54

WOOL, STRING, etc. — 1 kg thrums ... pp. 52·53

GLUE - powdered → ½ litre ... p. 52

CRAYPAS— 10 boxes of 12's ... p. 54

WIRE —1 bundle, aluminium — 1·5mm [100 lengths, 90cm] ... p. 52

    Also, if possible   —   CRÊPE PAPER – 2pkts - 2 colours ... p. 28

                              PASTELS – 4 boxes, block/round ... p. 49

                              CHARCOAL– 3 boxes, block ... pp. 49·51·55

                              INK – 1 btle, black ... p. 51

THE BARE BONES KIT

CHROMACRYL PAINT — BLUE or RED* ... pp. 42-46·48·53·54

    Also, if possible   —   CRAYPAS – 5pkts of 12's ... p. 54

SCAVENGE and SAVE { WOOL, STRING, etc. ... pp. 52·53

                      { WIRE [flexible] ... p. 52

MAKE YOUR OWN { FLOUR and WATER GLUE ... pp. 52

                   { CHARCOAL from burnt wood. pp. 49·51·55

THE *running on* ... THIN AIR KIT

CHROMACRYL PAINT — BLUE or RED* [yellow is too light] ... pp. 42-46·48·53·54

SCAVENGE, SAVE AND MAKE YOUR OWN AS FOR ABOVE KITS

N.B. Teachers with expertise in weaving may require specific materials.

FOR ALL KITS
- collection of "lines" e.g. ropes, sticks, elastic, wire, etc. ... p. 8, 9, 22, 23
- cardboard /paper strips and off-cuts ... p. 52
- plastic scrapers e.g. bread-wrapping holders ⋈ for sgraffito ... p. 54

* Commercial names : Cool Yellow, Warm Red, Warm Blue, Black, White.

SECTION ONE

Awareness experiences

AIMS:
- to awaken an interest in line **for its own sake**
- to develop a **vocabulary** about line at all levels of awareness ~ physical to abstract

- FEELING LINE
- SEEING LINE
- INTEGRATED EXPERIENCES WITH LINE
- LANGUAGE OF LINE

RESOURCES

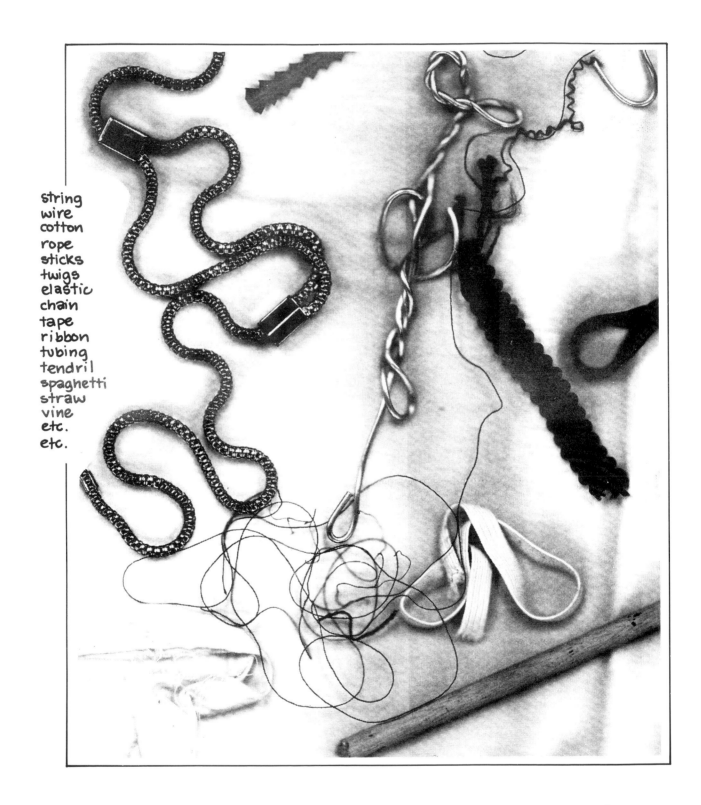

string
wire
cotton
rope
sticks
twigs
elastic
chain
tape
ribbon
tubing
tendril
spaghetti
straw
vine
etc.
etc.

Make a permanent collection of linear objects with a wide variety of thicknesses, lengths, flexibility, textures, and so on. This could start a lifetime hobby. Some teachers and artists have collections from all over the world. Students, parents and friends will enthusiastically join in collecting for you.

VOCABULARY BRAINSTORMING

BRING OUT YOUR COLLECTION OF LINES... ROPES, ELASTIC, VINES... DISTRIBUTE THEM AROUND THE CLASS. STUDENTS ARE BEST SEATED IN A CIRCLE ON THE FLOOR.

BRAINSTORM!

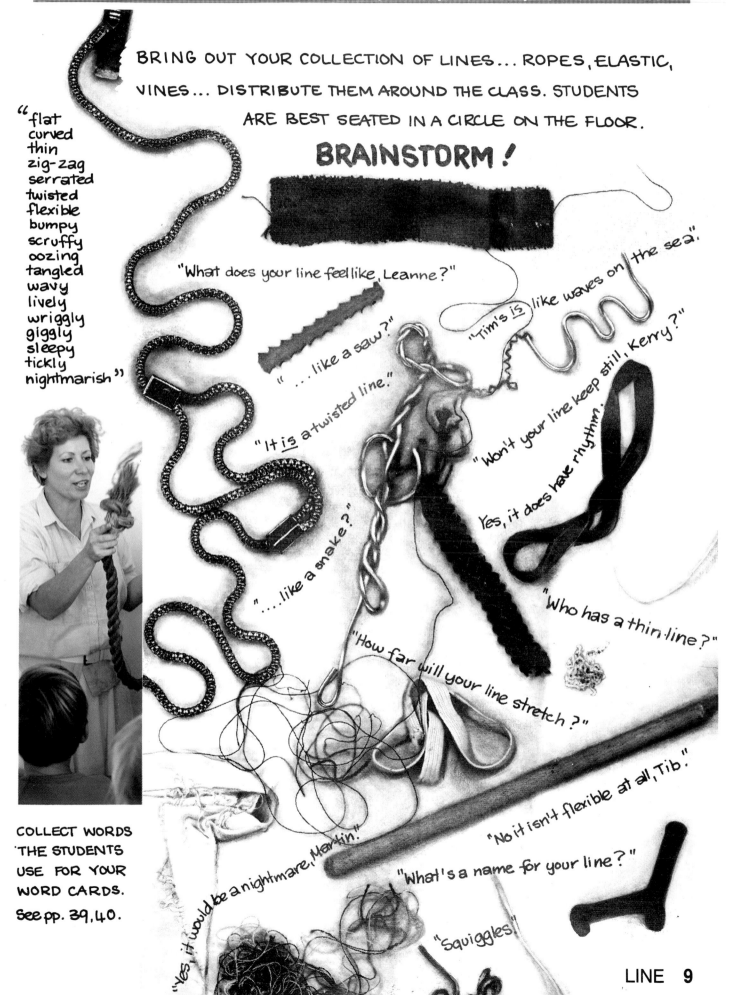

"flat
curved
thin
zig-zag
serrated
twisted
flexible
bumpy
scruffy
oozing
tangled
wavy
lively
wriggly
giggly
sleepy
tickly
nightmarish"

"What does your line feel like, Leanne?"

"Tim's is like waves on the sea?"

"... like a saw?"

"It is a twisted line."

"Won't your line keep still, Kerry?"

"Yes, it does have rhythm."

"... like a snake?"

"Who has a thin line?"

"How far will your line stretch?"

"No it isn't flexible at all, Tib."

"Yes, it would be a nightmare, Martin."

"What's a name for your line?"

"Squiggles"

COLLECT WORDS THE STUDENTS USE FOR YOUR WORD CARDS.
See pp. 39, 40.

PHYSICAL TYPES OF LINE

All lines can be described according to **abstract** qualities they are seen to possess by the viewer, e.g. dizzy, militant. The lines below are described according to their **physical** attributes only.

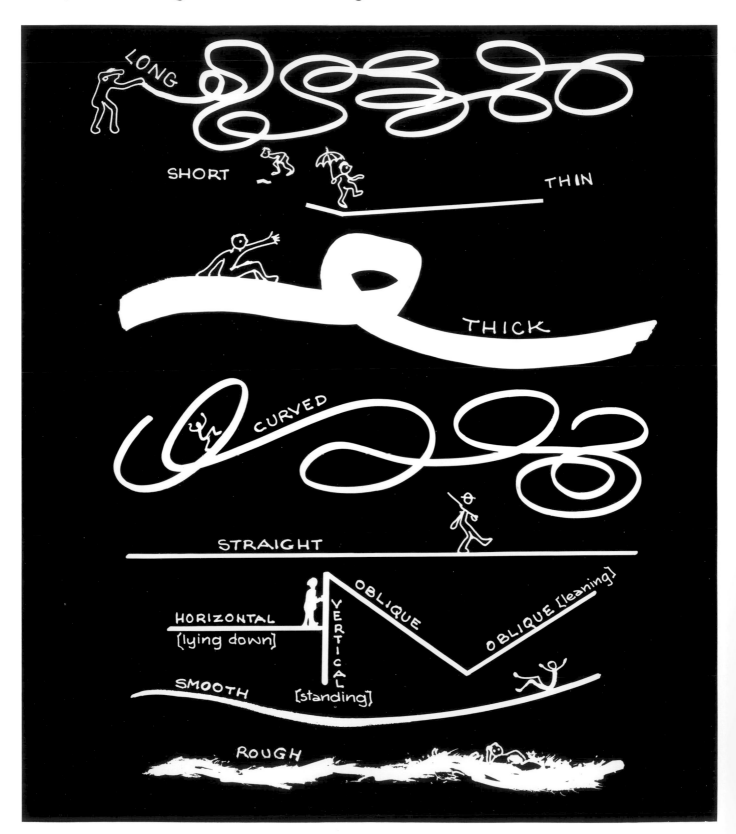

THE SEEING SAFARI

AIMS:
- to help the students learn to SEE, i.e. to see **more** than the mere physical presence of objects
- to develop further a **VOCABULARY** about line on all levels of awareness — physical to abstract

When going on safari in the schoolyard or down the road, point out any interesting or prominent lines and discuss them. What physical types are they [opposite page], and what words describe their character or movement? Write down these words for your collection. [see pp. 39-40.] Use them on word cards for displays. [see p.22]

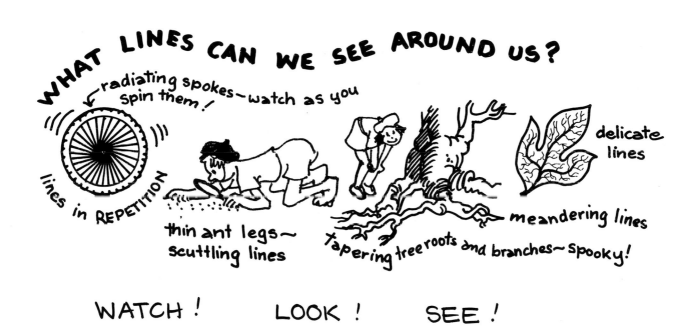

WATCH !   LOOK !   SEE !

DON'T HOLD BACK "BIG" WORDS. IF STUDENTS CAN <u>SEE</u> A TAPERING LINE, THEY MOST LIKELY CAN UNDERSTAND IT AND USE IT IN THEIR OWN WORK.

WORDS USED
ABOVE

thin
radiating
tapering
delicate
scuttling
meandering
spooky

THE SEEING SAFARI

...in the schoolyard

Photograph: Shelley Munster, Queensland

hints to foster new ideas

- Promote the idea that we are about to look on a **NEW WORLD**, one we haven't seen before. The whole place, wherever we are, will be riddled with lines ! Just look.

- Encourage NEW WORLD ideas. Suppose we came from another planet, had super-seeing, bulging eyes and fed only on lines ! Let's go foraging for food. Who has a favourite type? Anyone know the poem, "Nobody loves me, Everybody hates me, I'm going down the yard to eat ..." ?

- If all the lines we see could MOVE BY THEMSELVES, how would they move? Demonstrate some ~ posts hopping, tree roots slithering, telephone wires skipping [how about some "pepper"?]. If they all moved at once, what would the scene look like? If we put it to music, would we use rock 'n' roll, a lullaby ...?

- Find lines that are the SAME [REPETITION] or SIMILAR [in HARMONY], or very DIFFERENT [in CONTRAST]. See TEACHER'S GUIDE, pp. 42-47.

There is a whole new world to be discovered under the magnifying glass, exciting to all ages.

P.S. Encourage that sense of **HUMOUR**. It is one of the saving graces of the civilized world. Find it in the environment where you can.

MAKING THE MOST OF MEDIA

AUDIO-VISUAL RESOURCES:

Use an overhead projector creatively. Try two projectors and superimpose images. Tell stories with moving line, e.g. wool in water in a glass dish. Add colour with cellophane. Create linear pictures.

Investigate sources of videos, films, strips, etc. about LINE, or/and make some yourself. Ask school and community Libraries, Education Centres, Film centres, and so on.

Check the school television and radio broadcasts for Art programs. Timetables are usually available at the beginning of each year. Try to build up the school's resources.

WATCH AND DISCUSS.

STATIC RESOURCES:

See next page.

LOOK AND DISCUSS.

DISPLAY in the classroom, or elsewhere in the school ~

- photographs you, or others, have taken
- pictures from magazines
- newspaper photographs
- posters
- record covers, book covers, and so on.

You may have space for only **ONE** photograph in your classroom ~ fine!

It will have unrivalled status of importance ~ but do change it often.

classroom display   MEDIA

USE YOUR OWN PHOTOGRAPHS OR CUT OUT
PICTURES OF STRONG LINES FROM MAGAZINES.

Add your own touch

- Students could write poems or short
  descriptive pieces of prose about the
  lines in the photographs.
- Captions could be added.
- Add a quiz. Can you find lines that are
  parallel, radiating, tapering, wriggling,
  "roller-coastering"?

> zig-zag, zig-zag ~ the
> reflections ripple across the
> water, while the tall masts
> stand straight to attention.

RADIATING LINES ON A GUESS WHAT

Display some photographs upside down
or sideways, so that the **lines** are seen
more easily, rather than the subject.

MEDIA   **classroom display**

extract ideas from the media

Remember, artists extract their ideas from EVERYWHERE ~
including other artists. Build up your resources from all sources.

a) Cut photographs from newspapers ~ ones with strong lines. Make a
   MONTAGE by cutting out selected parts and pasting onto a background, overlapping where desired ~ perhaps joining the lines from
   one cut-out to those of another ~ to make a new original picture
   with an entirely new set of ideas put together. This activity
   usually produces very interesting results.

b) Use Nature study or other posters as a starter for seeing lines
   around us. Then go searching for the types of lines you have
   ◀ identified e.g. radiating [set some up in the room]

Photograph: John Turnock, Qld Department of Eduction

c) Cut out large photographs from magazines or
newspapers. Paste them onto a background. Using felt
pens, paint, or any other medium, draw over the
important lines – the ones that stand out. Add some, or
paint some out, to make a new picture. This helps the
student to be more aware of lines in photographs and
in the environment, as well as giving a starting point
for new ideas out of old.

Make your own set of slides or prints. The students can select lines from
around the school and work out a sequence, e.g. the shortest to the
longest; the thinnest to the thickest; contrasting to harmonious;
rhythmical, and in repetition. A title could be "KEEPING THE SCHOOL IN
LINE". Albums of prints are invaluable resources for displays.
See opposite page.

class album

COMPILE A CLASS ALBUM of your own photographs taken in the school grounds.

APPRECIATION IN THE WORLD OF ART

DISCUSS the Art works below in conjunction with the Student's Book, pp. 3, 8 and 11.

Courtesy of the Queensland Art Gallery

123.3 x 123.3 cm Gift of the Godfrey Rivers Trust through Daphne Mayo 1943

"THE CYPRIOT" by William DOBELL [1899-1970 AUST.]. Oil on canvas. This portrait is square~ an unusual choice. Feel how the lines lead your eyes in definite directions.

Each of these figures seems to be posing for the artist. Students could imitate these positions while the others draw them. Note the formal, symmetrical, radiating lines of the Cypriot. Contrast these with the flowing, dance-like pose of the Caryatid. Note how the Kabuki actor is stiff and tense in his straight, angular lines. Japanese artists are masters of Line, especially in their calligraphy.

37 x 25 cm Collection of the Japan Room, Town Gallery, Brisbane

Courtesy of Verlie Just

Wood-block print of a Kabuki actor by ASHIYUKI [circa 1820 JAPAN]. Ink on paper. A culturally traditional work.

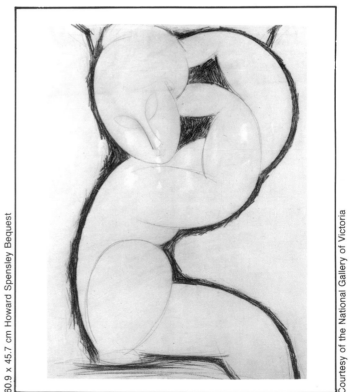

60.9 x 45.7 cm Howard Spensley Bequest

Courtesy of the National Gallery of Victoria

"CARYATID" by Amedeo MODIGLIANI [1884-1920 ITALY]. Drawing in blue chalk. Note the feeling of balance.

APPRECIATION IN THE WORLD OF ART

A batik cloth from Bali with traditional figures. Seepage through wax varies the colour of lines.

Aboriginal rock painting, N.T. Aust.

Architect: Frank Lloyd Wright U.S.A.

Dome of Guggenheim Museum, New York.

Stela of Nebuhetep (detail). Limestone. Egyptian (segment) New Kingdom Dynasty XIX, Reign of Rameses II, 1304-1237 B.C.

Presented by British School of Archaeology in Egypt 1921

Courtesy of the National Gallery of Victoria

Ancient Egyptian intaglio [grooved] carving.

See how RADIATING, PARALLEL, CONCENTRIC and SPIRAL linear patterns feature in the above works. Turn to pp. 56-58 for practical experiences.

APPRECIATION IN THE WORLD OF ART

This painted, low-relief sculptured wall at Tiger Balm Gardens in
Singapore is seething with curving lines of serpents and turbulent waves.
The total effect of harmony of similar lines is a powerful one, given extra
"fury" by the subject matter. What magnificent symphonic music it would make!

APPRECIATION IN THE WORLD OF ART

bring Appreciation to life

Being creative with someone else's creative work is nothing new. Think what has been done with the "Mona Lisa"! John Ruskin, the English critic, expounded, along with others after him, that originality emerges only out of tradition, as we have seen with the Australian Aboriginal culture. Agree or not, we certainly can make the work of others the starting point for our own ideas.

Now, what can we do with William Dobell's "The Cypriot" [p.18] that will also increase our appreciation of it?

a) <u>ARRANGE SEVERAL PORTRAITS TOGETHER</u> [any will do]

e.g.

THE CYPRIOT by William Dobell	MONA LISA by Leonardo da Vinci	GERTRUDE STEIN by Pablo Picasso

In the Tate Gallery, London, a drama group re-enacts the story of the Picasso painting behind them.

i) Discuss and write <u>CHARACTER STUDIES</u>. Which one is boss? Who is shy?

ii) Act out a <u>TABLEAU</u>. Three students sit in front of the class, imitating the expressions. What is each one thinking? How would each one react, if told, "There is a spider on your shoulder!"?

b) <u>CREATE A PLAY</u> to describe a story fitting any painting you know. If living in a city, ask the Art Gallery if any plays will be enacted about paintings. Offer to produce one with the students. Small, country galleries would probably welcome such an interesting event, be it ever so humble.

MAKING A LINE DISPLAY

LINES ON CENTRE STAGE

sticks   string   elastic   tendrils   vines
wool   cane   reeds
wire   grass   sea-weed   spaghetti

... on a table, bench or shelf, ideally with a display board above

magnificent   super   marvellous   fragile   radiating   crinkled   giggling   splendid   stiff

YUMMY

If having a display board made, try glueing hessian or cloth over Caneite, or other fibrous material.

No space in the classroom?

> TRY... a "line a day". Each student or group brings
> along samples of natural or man-made linear
> objects to display to the rest of the class, like
> a Morning Talk or Show and Tell.
>
> ... arranging displays in the Library, the Ad-
> ministration Block, the Staff Room, or in some
> corridor for the whole school to see.

Also — flat, linear objects come out well on the **photocopier.**
These may be displayed more easily and happily than
the object itself, particularly if the object is "precious".

MAKING A LINE DISPLAY

WHAT'S NEW, PUSSY CAT?

If a display is left up for too long, it dies.

Select several linear objects and arrange them to mean something.
[Don't forget humour.] Add titles or captions ~ a little creative
writing for the day.

Let the students draw the cut-outs ~ not copied. Accept _their_ cat.

Add a palm
frond tail

THE CAT WHO TOLD TALL TALES — LIKE PINOCCHIO

Add grass whiskers

"SCHMUFFLEMEEOW"

Add the crinkled
strip of paper

ON THE CRINKLED SEA

THE BULLY

Arrange so that the
large stick is "chasing"
the vine tendril

Make a pattern or pleasing
arrangement with several
of the linear objects.

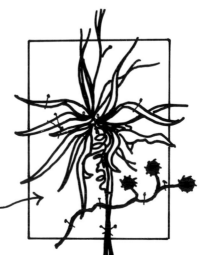

Add a piece of
coloured cardboard

LINES IN CONTRAST

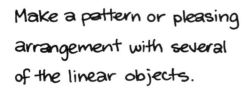

RECORDING LINES FROM LIFE

See TEACHER'S GUIDE, pp. 22-27.

JUST LINES ~ NOT A PICTURE OR DRAWING OF OBJECTS.

The easiest and most valuable lesson of all!

The teacher's task? Simply accompany the class happily around the chosen environment, e.g. the school yard, while the students find their own lines and draw them as a collection on paper, in pencil — arrangement is not important. Exclude any really disruptive students. It will not harm their artistic development to miss out on the activity. Let the others be free of an irritable teacher! It will probably only happen once, this way.

Select a student to **photograph** some of the lines for your resource collection ~ black and white film will do. Try some close-ups. How about experimenting through a magnifying glass, kept absolutely still?

Cameras are "miracle machines".
Put them to work for you.

DISPLAY and **DISCUSS** the above drawings [and photographs?] under a heading such as ~

BEWARE! LINES ON LOOSE AROUND SCHOOL!

RECORDING LINES FROM LIFE

CAPTURING LINES

Just lines — not the objects themselves.

RECORDING LINES FROM LIFE

NOW FIND A SUBJECT WITH STRONG LINES TO DRAW

Above, a Principal works with her class, drawing the lines of the school.

YEARS 6 and 7

BEING LINE IN DRAMA

✳ let's be line

<u>Needed</u> : Space — and bodies

HEY PRESTO ! ✳✳ YOU ARE A ....

SIMON SAYS .... YOU ARE A ....

straight line ; curved line ; vertical , horizontal and oblique line , all at once ; straight <u>and</u> curved line ; long line ...

CHARADES .... what sort of line am I?

.. what sort of line are you?

delicate ; tapering ; stiff ; stubborn ; shy ?

CAN YOU MOVE LIKE A LINE THAT IS ... tired; graceful ; nervous ; haughty ; angry ; monotonous ?

NOW, LINES, LET ME SEE YOU ....

zig-zag like a ski-er ; zoom like a rocket ; ooze like syrup ;   dissolve like smoke ?!

CAN TWO OF YOU BE ....

an asterisk ; the letter E ; a fan ?

CAN THREE OF YOU BE ....

a flower opening to the sun ?

WHAT CAN THE WHOLE CLASS BE ?

WATCHING LINE

✳ let's dance

- Form **DANCE GROUPS** ~ "The Swirling Whirligigs"... "The Red Rotisseries"..."The Jagged Jerkers"...

Work out a sequence of movements with long scarves or streamers ~ a good lunch-time activity. Some groups spend hours practising in their own time. Very intricate linear sequences can be obtained from light, sheer materials. Remember REPETITION is the key-note of pattern. Add music.

- These routines could be recorded on **VIDEO**, added to by other classes, and kept for resources. Still photographs ~ prints or slides ~ could also be made.

- Select small groups to work out sequences of movement such as lines FOLDING UP; COILING UP; UNRAVELLING; ROTATING; RADIATING; UNDULATING; OOZING. Try some PERISTALTIC MOTION! ...like a worm .....
..... students hold hands in a line and move arms in sequence. Any "rap dancers" or "moon walkers"? Add music?
[Make sure these routines or dances are done in groups so that students are **WATCHING** moving lines.]

WATCHING LINE

✳ let's use the video camera

THINK... •• what line **moves** by itself ?...[worm], when switched on ?...[ferris wheel], when pushed ?...[ski-trail], when pedalled ?...

MAKE A VIDEO OF INTERESTING PATTERNS OF MOVING LINE — e.g.

a) While down at the local creek, drawing from life, at the swimming pool, or near a puddle, throw a stone in the water and watch ~ are the ripples concentric ? the reflections zig-zag ?

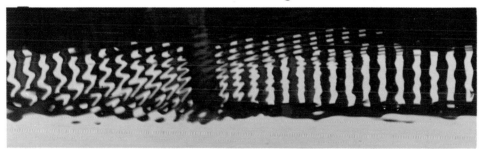

b) Rotate a disc of cardboard on a pencil. Draw lines on the disc. Try different lines at different speeds. Video.

c) shadow play ~ use a sheet/screen and OVERHEAD PROJECTOR light. students between the screen and projector, hold up and turn springs, wire spirals, curled strips of paper ~ try two or three bicycle wheels overlapping ~ watch the interplay of radiating spokes! Make your own "wheels" from cardboard and wool. Spin them on a taut string. Video.

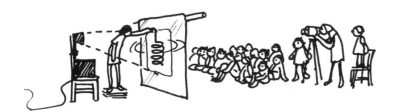

Also, wriggle some wool on the horizontal glass of the projector. Try other lines also — sticks, ribbons, etc.

WATCHING LINE

✳ let's paint

a) Painting the rhythms of music in line can be an exciting venture with small groups. Tape a long sheet of paper [smaller sheets joined if necessary] to an exterior wall or "wet-area" wall—one metre by four metres would be plenty. One student walking alongside another, paint pot in one hand, brush in the other, moves along the paper, from left to right, drawing to the up and down rhythms of the music as if conducting. It could look rather like a graph sheet. You could video the finished work, moving from one end to the other, to the accompaniment of the music.

Photograph: Shelley Munster, Queensland

b) Make your own "T.V. Set" and "video tape". Only a cardboard carton and piece of doweling or other rod are required. Paint the lines to the music, then put it through the "machine" to the music.

Rotate doweling to wind up paper

✳ listening is an active activity

BRING A PILLOW!

IF the class cannot listen actively while lying down comfortably on the floor, and then discussing what they hear in terms of **line**, e.g. the up and down progression of notes, or an aesthetic effect such as gliding line, or jerky, zig-zag line . . .

THEN add some **action** requiring listening, e.g.

- for "DANCE OF THE REED PIPES" from "The Nutcracker Suite" by Tchaikovsky, or other music that "climbs" or "falls" . . . pretend to play the piano; or use your fingers, climbing UP and down . . . for lines going high and low.

- for "TWITTERING MACHINE" by Schuller . . .

  pretend to be a wind-up toy "twittering machine" ~ in groups ~ arms rotating for the winding up, etc. Many bodies belonging to the one machine give the arrangement a feeling of UNITY. [Seek out the painting of the same name, by the swiss painter, Paul Klee, that inspired Schuller to write the music. Students will enjoy the fun of both the painting and music.] After watching other groups in the class perform their "machines", the children may like to develop this activity adding cardboard cut-out machine parts to the action, and drawing or painting their idea of the machine while the music is playing, keeping lines SUITABLE for the sounds.

N.B. See TEXTURE, p.48, re source of suggested music pieces.

LISTENING TO LINE

- for **"THE SWAN"** from "Carnival of the Animals" by Saint-Saëns, or other music with a smooth flow ...
  pretend to **glide** around the room ~ as a hang-glider, a glider 'possum, a paper plane, a dandelion seed in the wind, an eagle, etc. How else could you move to this music? Can you feel the gliding lines?

- for **"BERCEUSE"** from "The Firebird Suite" by Stravinsky ...
  Students could try to imagine why the music is so **sad**.
  What could have happened in the story? Who is sad?
  Can you feel the sad lines? Is there a happy ending?

- for **"BARCAROLLE"** by Offenbach, or other music with the quality of calm ...
  listen for the feeling of **peace** ~ definitely music for resting ~ heads down or lie down, and let the music drift around the room. Can you feel the peaceful lines?

- for **SYMPHONY N° 5 - FIRST MOVEMENT** by Schubert or any other purely instrumental music ...
  just listen to the pure sound of music, then ask, do you like the music? Do you think it is "good" or "bad"? Is it beautiful, or ordinary and mundane?
  Try to develop a vocabulary for aesthetic judgements.
  Accept the student's own vocabulary — and then EXTEND IT.

"GRATING PLEASANT"
LOVELY NICE SUPERB
STIMULATING MONOTONOUS "
AWFUL
CACOPHONOUS
"SOUL-DESTROYING SPLENDID
PEDESTRIAN PRETTY

"RIPPER EXCELLENT"
TERRIFIC
TOPS SUPER FAR OUT
BORRRING UNREAL
"COOL GREAT YUK
YEAH, MAN BEAUT "
FANTASMAGORICAL

For more words, and some professional jargon, search out the reviews on Music, Art and Sculpture in newspapers.

CREATING LINE WITH INSTRUMENTS

❋ give line a new dimension

Let's give line another way of being "alive", e.g.

- for PHYSICAL TYPES : long, short, thin, thick, etc. [See p. 10] try a long horizontal line ~ one long sustained note on an organ or recorder ~ or didgeridoo! Ask a student to draw the sound on a blackboard.

one long breath

[or just whistle.]

- for a line "LIKE A TRAIN" : try a repeated two-note drone on a xylophone, accompanied by a "chugga-chugga" :‖ [repeated] . . . on the maracas. Does it sound zig-zag? jagged?

chugg-a, chugg-a, chugg-a . . . .

- for a line "LIKE (something) JUMPING" : try bouncing a beater from high to low, high to low, on a xylophone [or on bottles filled to different heights with water]. The jumping effect is more easily felt if only one beater is used.

- for a line "LIKE IMPATIENCE" : try some loud, up-and-down-the-piano chords [notes played together], any notes, any where, in a hurry ~ the more discord the better. [No piano? Try banging on home-made "drums" - tins, sauce-pans, etc. with spoons!]

CREATING LINE WITH INSTRUMENTS

"LIKE NONSENSE" —

Try sounds played in a a haphazard manner at various tempos [speeds] with varied dynamics [loud and soft] on a variety of instruments.

Use silence to break up the sounds into "groups" and "surprises". The humour will be appreciated by the students.

PURE ABSTRACTION — Select a student to make some "beautiful lines" on a favourite instrument, with a few phrases of melody or some rhythmic patterns, if the student understands those terms. No-one else needs to like them. Aesthetics is like that.

<u>N.B.</u> In "pure abstract" music there is no reference to anything in real life, such as trains, machines, etc. The subject is simply the effect of the sounds in their own right. This type of music is called ABSOLUTE MUSIC, and is the auditory equivalent of Abstract Art in which the subject is the effect produced by the arrangement of the Elements in their own right. Titles usually indicate if the music is "absolute" ~ sonatas, symphonies, concertos are usually "absolute". Music about "real-life things" is called PROGRAM MUSIC and has titles such as "Twittering Machine", "In the Hall of the Mountain King", "Peter and the Wolf" and "The Blue Danube".

Folk who cannot accept abstraction in art, e.g. as in Abstract Art, are conditioned to reject it. Thank heavens Music and Literature haven't been put into cages marked "PHYSICAL RECORDS ONLY"! These eyes were made for seeing, but everyone's mind and senses "see" <u>more</u> than the mere physical and it <u>can</u> be made visual. This is what "Running on Rainbows" is all about.

CREATING LINE FROM SOUND

❇ more activities with line and sound

a) Behind a small "stage curtain" [any cloth will do], produce a sound made by any objects, or object, that can be blown, beaten, or plucked into doing so ~ but not a recognized instrument. Ask the students to imagine the "instrument" and draw it. Then draw the sound coming from the instrument, as it would look if it could be seen. Try to keep the sound consistent. [students can prepare such "instruments" at home.]

b) Play some music with strong melody [easy to sing] several times, then ask students to draw, with the music, the patterns the music makes. Assist by suggesting a few possible qualities music can have, e.g. jerkiness, swirling flow. Remember, the key-note of pattern is REPETITION. Music is full of it. The work below was illustrating the pattern in the "William Tell Overture" by Rossini ~ used for a coffee advertisement on television! Try "Can Can" by Rossini [based on "Can Can" by Offenbach], and "Changing of the Guard" by Bizet, or other music with strong rhythm.

Song of the Coffee.

N.B. See TEXTURE, p.48, re source of suggested music pieces.

WRITING ABOUT LINE

❋ getting words into line

a) **POEMS**: Try some **"STARTERS"**, e.g. the student completes ~

"A line can be ... [e.g. a silver trail,

Made by a wandering garden snail.] "

"Some lines are ... [e.g. grumpy

Some lines are ... tight.

Others are ... wrigglers,

And ... eager to fight.] "

b) **STORIES**: i) Take a chalk line on an adventure around a concrete or bitumen area. Students take turns to draw the line on the ground, around posts, down the drain, to the tuckshop, along the cracks ... As they draw, the students describe the line's adventures ~ what happened down the drain ... [see opposite page ~ teacher is the scribe.]

ii) Another story could be of the Aesop fable type ~ *How* the line got its prickles ... found its niche ... found its way home ... lost its length "

c) **SCRIPTS**: For a play, video, shadow-play, or puppets, try conversations between, e.g. Fat Line and Skinny Line, Long Line and Short Line, Thin Line and Thick Line, with contrast of emotions such as pride and shame, frustration and calm, domination and fear, built into the dramatic situation. Hand puppets would do. See COLOUR, p.44.

d) **SNIPPETS**: e.g. sentences or captions for Notice Boards ~

LIVELY LINES LIKE TO LAUGH LOUDLY

SLOW DOWN LINES CROSSING

LAZY LINES LIKE TO LURK IN LANEWAYS

WRITING ABOUT LINE

✳ taking line on an adventure

"Once upon a time a line went on an exciting adventure... he's going up and down... going to the shop... squiggling... to the park to play on the swing and now he's dizzy... he's going to the doctor... going zig-zag... bumpy and curly...

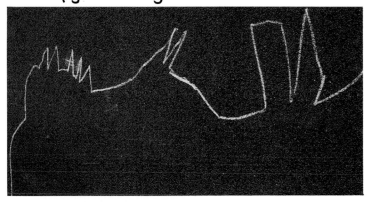

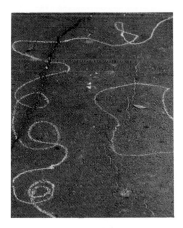

he's speeding now... wriggling like a worm... he's going to the doctor again... he's in bed... he's going out in a car ...in a spiral... he's going home riding his bike, looping"...

As each child drew an extension to the line, the teacher wrote down the child's verbal addition of the story — a truly **significant** line!

MAKING USE OF TECHNOLOGY   computer

✳ exploring line on the computer

Can you make rhythmic patterns by repeating curved lines? Do they appear to be moving? See p.7. Also, find some of the linear paintings by the British artist, Bridgit Riley, such as "Current".

YEAR 7

Take some sketches from outside in the school yard [perhaps some done during an outdoor sketching day], or in the room. Translate these onto the screen. Re-arrange the lines, repeat them to make patterns, change their thickness . . . explore.

Peninsula School, Mt. Eliza, Victoria.

COLLECTION AND DISPLAY OF WORDS

COLLECTION AND DISPLAY

✳ This is a `BIG` MOMENT ~ a tally of the vocabulary that has been collected so far.

LET'S CHECK AND ORGANISE A READY- REFERENCE BANK FOR THE FUTURE

Collect all the words and good phrases USED, HEARD or SEEN and add any more you wish from

- your collected list
- a dictionary
- the Art program
- a thesaurus

OR memory

 BEST IDEA...If you haven't already done so, put these words onto WORD CARDS for future resources, displays, and so on.

SEE NEXT PAGE.

Now DISPLAY ALL THE WORDS AND GOOD PHRASES FOR THE CLASS TO SEE.

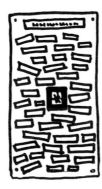

COLLECTION AND DISPLAY OF WORDS

some words related to line

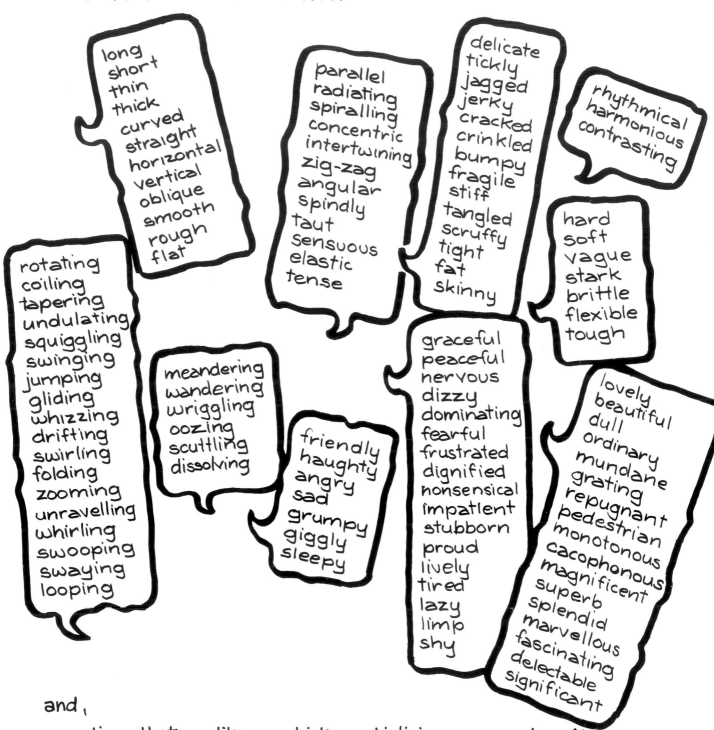

long
short
thin
thick
curved
straight
horizontal
vertical
oblique
smooth
rough
flat

parallel
radiating
spiralling
concentric
intertwining
zig-zag
angular
spindly
taut
sensuous
elastic
tense

delicate
tickly
jagged
jerky
cracked
crinkled
bumpy
fragile
stiff
tangled
scruffy
tight
fat
skinny

rhythmical
harmonious
contrasting

hard
soft
vague
stark
brittle
flexible
tough

rotating
coiling
tapering
undulating
squiggling
swinging
jumping
gliding
whizzing
drifting
swirling
folding
zooming
unravelling
whirling
swooping
swaying
looping

meandering
wandering
wriggling
oozing
scuttling
dissolving

friendly
haughty
angry
sad
grumpy
giggly
sleepy

graceful
peaceful
nervous
dizzy
dominating
fearful
frustrated
dignified
nonsensical
impatient
stubborn
proud
lively
tired
lazy
limp
shy

lovely
beautiful
dull
ordinary
mundane
grating
repugnant
pedestrian
monotonous
cacophonous
magnificent
superb
splendid
marvellous
fascinating
delectable
significant

and,

    ...lines that are like...whiskers, whirligigs, syrup and smoke

    ...lines that move like...a worm, ferris-wheel, train, machine, hang-

          glider, paper-plane, an eagle, and a dandelion seed in

          the wind

    ...and lines that... are made by a wandering garden snail

HOW DOES YOUR COLLECTION COMPARE?

SECTION TWO
Practical experiences

Who needs an expensive easel?!

Building "Crystal Palace"

● <u>EXPERIENCE IN THE MOST SUITABLE MEDIUM</u> ~ <u>PAINT</u>*

    • EXPERIMENTAL "PLAY"

    • DIRECTED EXPERIENCE — note on Demonstrations; Wall chart

    • APPLIED EXPERIENCE

● <u>OTHER MEDIA AND TECHNIQUES</u> : charcoal drawing; drawing from life; environmental weaving; paper and cardboard construction; wool collage; wire sculpture; printing [block, string-on-block, string pull]; sgraffito; monoprinting; frottage; linear designs; designing

● "DOING YOUR OWN THING" TIME

    ✱ CHROMACRYL PAINT IS THE BEST AVAILABLE STUDENT PAINT THAT CAN PRODUCE THE THICK TEXTURES OF OIL PAINTS, THE FLAT TEXTURES OF POSTER PAINTS, AND THE TRANSPARENCY OF WATER-COLOURS.

Paint......lines, lines, lines

~ with the opportunity for students to make noise, move around, talk, and watch other students.

They usually learn much from each other in this session.

To set up for painting, see TEACHER'S GUIDE, pp. 62·63.

THE TEACHER'S ROLE ~

- To OBSERVE and LISTEN to the students without giving direction; asking questions to elicit what is happening and why. Be an interested observer. Observe the responses and reactions of students to each other and to their work, the intensity of their involvement, their degree of co-operation and individuality, their tendencies to imitate, and their inhibitions or otherwise. Observe the variety of activities, biasses, preferences and attitudes. Listen to the critical evaluations of their own work and others' and the vocabulary used.

- To PRAISE and ENCOURAGE at every opportunity, to help develop essential confidence for future work. Disruptive behaviour, of course, is in a different category, not to be confused with "freedom of artistic expression".

- To EVALUATE the levels of awareness the class or individuals have reached in their use of line, the range of their vocabulary related to line, and their degree of creativity. Here is an opportunity to decide which areas of awareness require further direction, correction or extension. Also, here is a time for the students to discover facts about the materials and equipment that teachers often take for granted that the students know — for instance, that paints change colour when mixed.

Working outside on large sheets of paper is highly appropriate for exper-imental and exploratory work as students feel a sense of freedom. It is not essential of course, and the classroom is quite suitable. In fact, some tech-niques are best done on a horizontal surface with small pieces of paper, e.g. printing lines with painted string between two sheets of paper pressed to-gether. If possible, provide the students with other materials that lend them-selves to line-making, such as rollers, sticks, forks, combs, plastic scrapers, etc. The girls above are exploring line-making with brushes, scrapers and rollers.

EXPERIMENTAL "PLAY"

painting

with **PAINT** — on large
sheets of paper, big and
small brushes — just **LINES**

painting techniques

DIRECTED EXPERIENCE

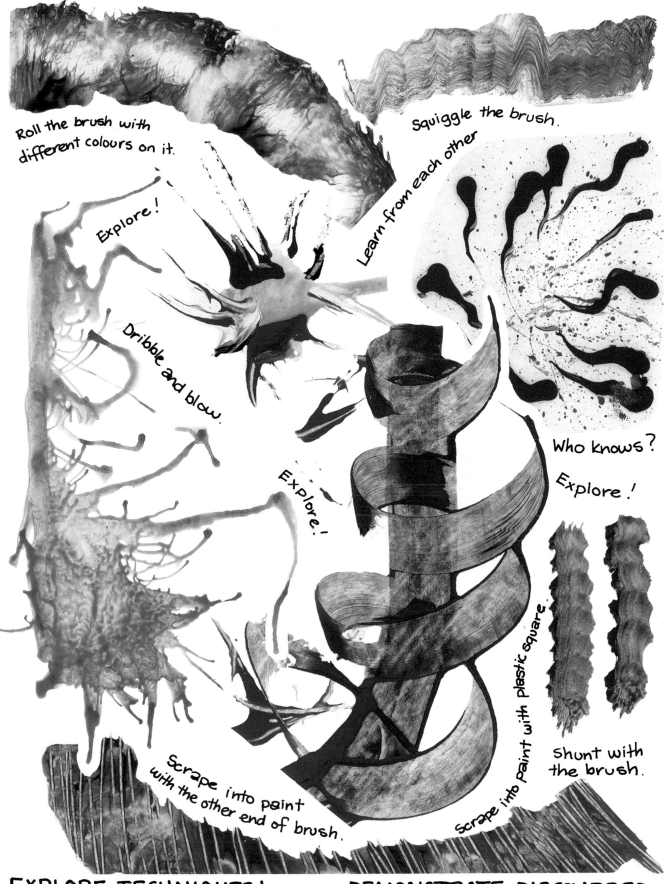

Roll the brush with different colours on it.

Squiggle the brush.

Explore!

Learn from each other

Dribble and blow.

Explore!

Who knows?

Explore!

Scrape into paint with the other end of brush.

Scrape into paint with plastic square.

Shunt with the brush.

EXPLORE TECHNIQUES! TECHNIQUES FOR ALL TO TRY!

DEMONSTRATE DISCOVERED

See also, COLOUR, Activity 17, pp. 33, 34.

DIRECTED EXPERIENCE

Photograph: Betty Baram, Qld Department of Education

Photograph: Betty Baram, Qld Department of Education

note on Demonstrations

THE GOOD : A demonstration is better than a thousand words. It brings the subject alive immediately and lessens the possibility of misconceptions.

THE BAD : Students might just copy without exploring or creating. So, demonstrate, then actively encourage experimentation. Put your own work out of sight if necessary. If a subject has been used, suggest other subjects.

In the photographs above, the teacher has used flowers for a subject to demonstrate the "blob-and-dribble" technique. Seeing the end product of such a simple technique is a lesson in itself. The "blob-and-dribble", often denigrated as "kindergarten play", when applied skilfully to a subject, becomes "professional". Note how well the child above has copied the teacher, adding printing and scraping. It is important now to ensure the child explores her own techniques for this subject, or else she may paint flowers only in this way, forever.

A WALL CHART DISCUSSION

A WALL CHART

Cut out and glue onto a chart, samples of different lines — at least one from each student. This may seem a tiresome task, but the chart will be a resource for years to come. In a class discussion, decide on words to describe each. Try to use some interesting and new words as well. Don't forget the humorous and poetic. The chart could be displayed in the Library or other classrooms.

As well as using your own chart, borrow one from another class for discussion.

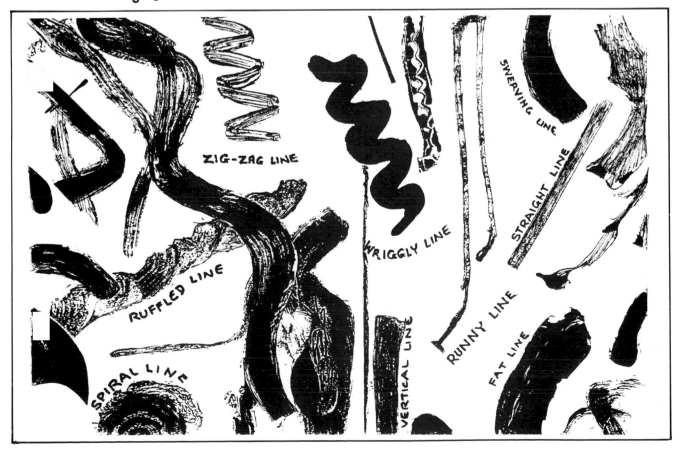

ZIG-ZAG LINE

SWERVING LINE

STRAIGHT LINE

WRIGGLY LINE

RUFFLED LINE

RUNNY LINE

FAT LINE

VERTICAL LINE

SPIRAL LINE

APPLIED EXPERIENCE

LET'S APPLY THE TECHNIQUES

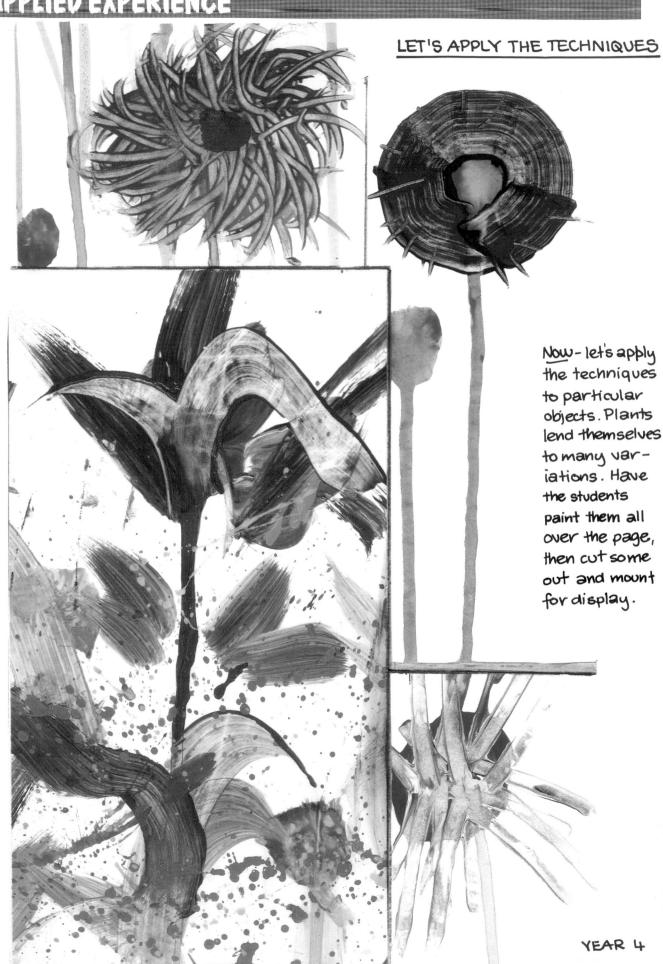

Now - let's apply the techniques to particular objects. Plants lend themselves to many variations. Have the students paint them all over the page, then cut some out and mount for display.

YEAR 4

YEAR 7

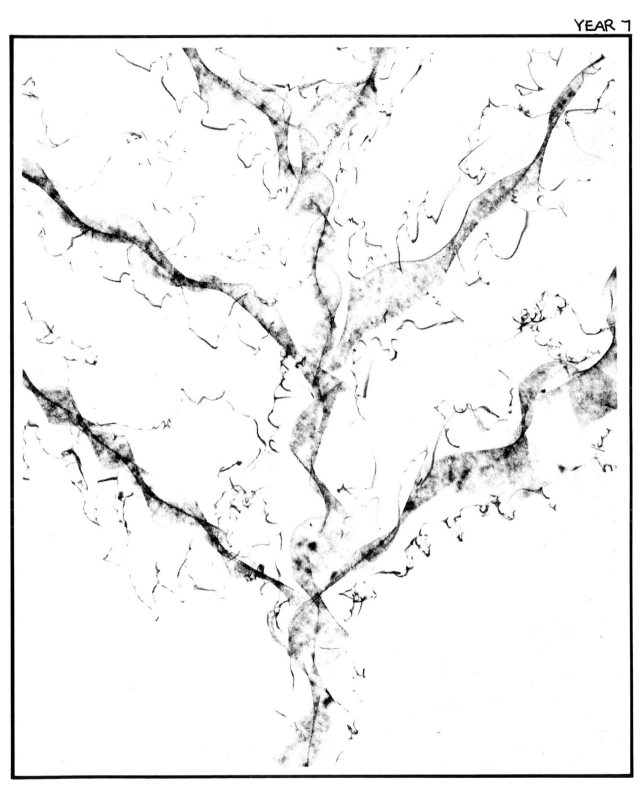

CHARCOAL DRAWING — Only the square-sided, compressed charcoal
will produce effects such as above. Pastels also lend themselves to
expressive linework. Try light colours on a dark background.
See TONE, Activities 18, 19, pp. 26-28.

DRAWING FROM LIFE   pencil

...TEACHES US TO **SEE!!!**

The only requirement is concentration.
SO, select interesting subjects – e.g. you!

In this drawing of ▶
the teacher by a
Year 2 child, the
figure has taken
second place to the
blackboard, shelves
and cupboard behind.
Imagine the level of
concentration reached
by this child.

YEAR 2

▲ This drawing of the teacher
shows how practice in seeing
lines has paid off. Notice the
overlapping of the feet, indicat-
ing a feeling of depth of space.

This interesting ▶
drawing by a Year
5 child, of the house
next to the school,
was done without
looking down at the
paper, [the child's
own idea, although
such drawings had
been done in class.]

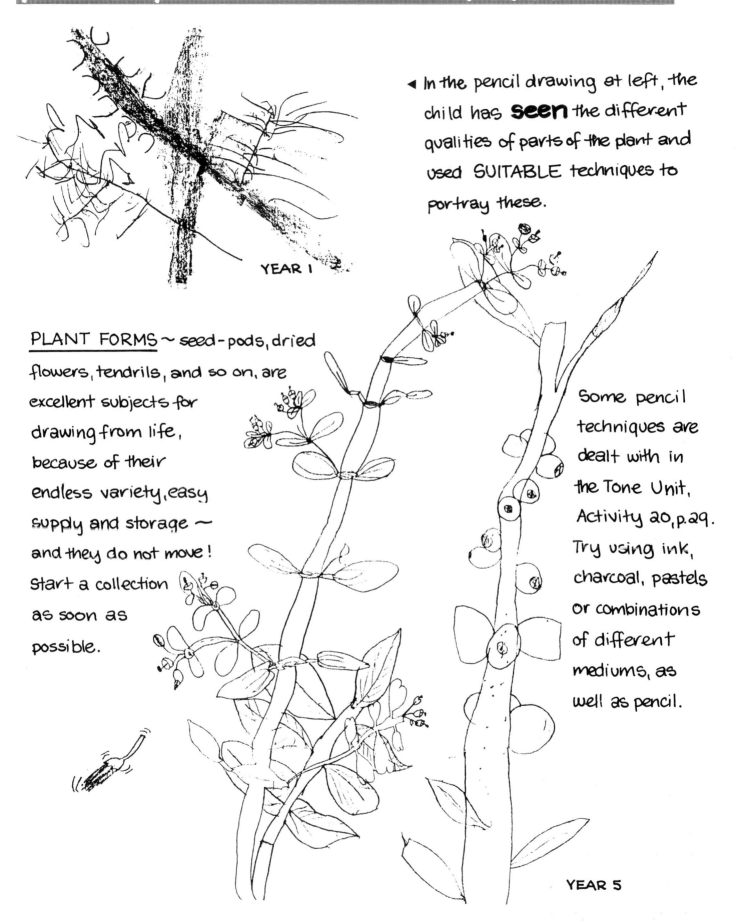

YEAR 1

◄ In the pencil drawing at left, the child has **seen** the different qualities of parts of the plant and used SUITABLE techniques to portray these.

PLANT FORMS ~ seed-pods, dried flowers, tendrils, and so on, are excellent subjects for drawing from life, because of their endless variety, easy supply and storage ~ and they do not move! Start a collection as soon as possible.

Some pencil techniques are dealt with in the Tone Unit, Activity 20, p.29. Try using ink, charcoal, pastels or combinations of different mediums, as well as pencil.

YEAR 5

REMEMBER — Always praise genuine attempts. Encourage every student.

FOUR LINEAR ACTIVITIES

A whole school group activity

20 environmental weaving

Wool, string, nylon . . .
a "crystal palace"
under the school steps.
Between trees is also
suitable. No special
knots are required.

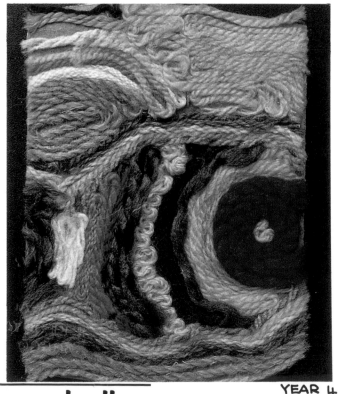

21 paper and cardboard construction

Note the RHYTHM
flowing throughout the
construction. Adhesive
tape was used for
joins. Explore other
joining methods.

YEAR 6

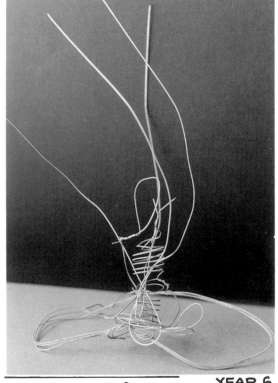

YEAR 4

22 wool collage —glued onto card

YEAR 6

23 wire sculpture "LOBSTER"

PRINTING

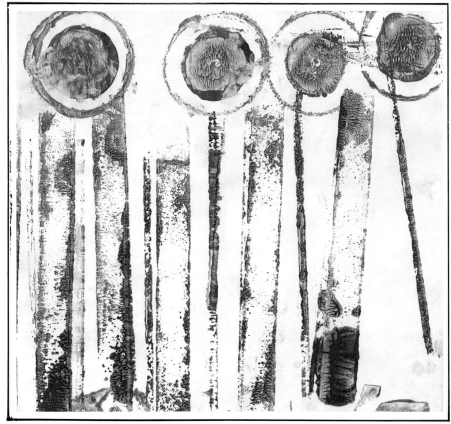

24 block print

Can be done with any objects ~ lids, paddle-pop sticks, cut vegetables, fingers, pieces of poly-styrene, crumpled rag, sponges, and so on. Block printing is an interesting medium to introduce or consolidate sequencing in the area of mathematics.

YEAR 3

25 string-on block

YEAR 5

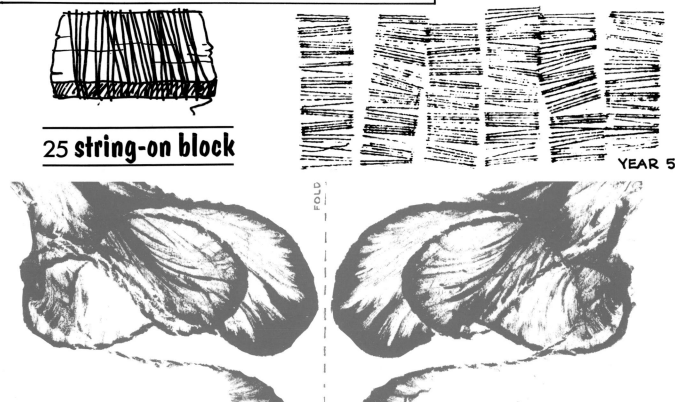

FOLD

26 string pull print

Dip string into Chromacryl, place between folded paper, press down with one hand, pull the string out with the other.

N.B. CHROMACRYL PAINTS POSSESS AN EXCELLENT CONSISTENCY FOR PRINTING.

MONOPRINT

See also, COLOUR, p.51.

YEAR 3

27 sgraffito

This is an **exciting** technique! Cover the page heavily with Craypas or other crayon, in any colours, in any arrangement. Paint over completely with Chromacryl in any colour, but black _is_ effective. While wet, scrape into the paint ~ plastic bread-wrapper holders are ideal. For an engraving effect, let paint dry first and scrape with a pointed instrument.

N.B. Chromacryl paint has the best consistency for sgraffito as it is thick enough to cover the oil-based crayon. Other paints are often too thin and the oil resists them.

YEAR 3

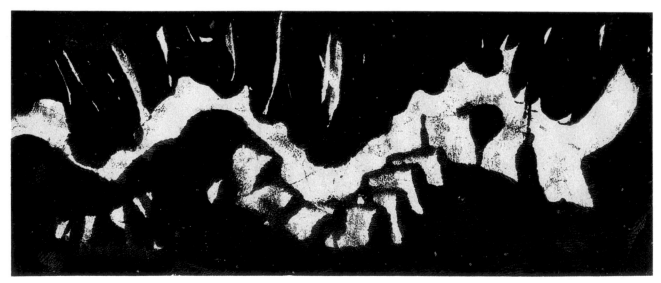

28 monoprint
Simply press paper [butcher paper will do] onto the wet sgraffito. Again, chromacryl will hold its shape and not splutter.

FROTTAGE

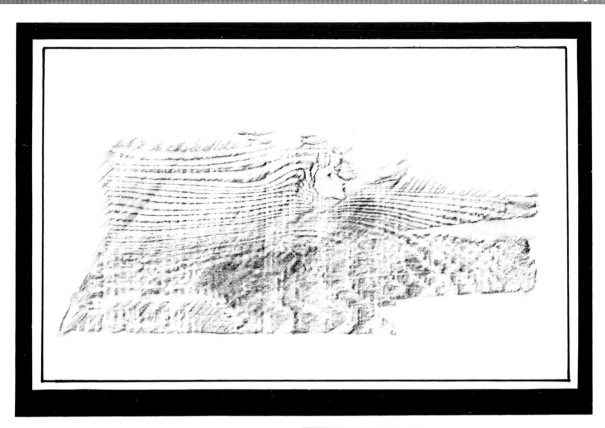

YEAR 7

29 frottage

The frottage, or "rubbing", above was made with pencil on butcher paper over rough timber. The face was discovered later.

Pencil over thin strips of cardboard or string is also effective. Cardboard that has been scored with scissors will produce a negative (white) line. Try both negative and positive together, i.e. pencil over cotton lying on scored cardboard.

Charcoal is softer than pencil and will produce effective frottages, although it is more likely to fill the grooves if pressed too hard, so that the lines are lost.

LINEAR DESIGN   pencil

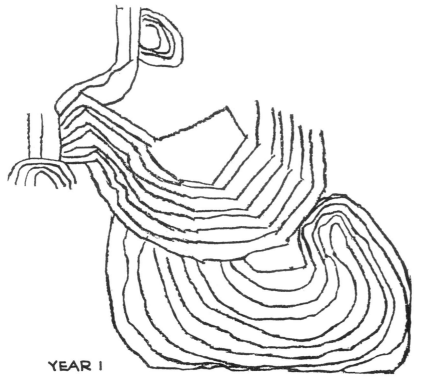

YEAR 1

DESIGN IS . . . .
deliberate arrangement.

30 designing · pencil

The designs on this page follow a deliberate arrangement
~sets of PARALLEL lines.
Demonstrate first on the blackboard, then rub it out. Here is
a fun opportunity for young children to use rulers if they wish.
Year 1 children understand

parallel lines and can use the words, even if they forget them soon after. Some
may remember the words, but all, most likely, will remember the way to draw
them.

YEAR 2

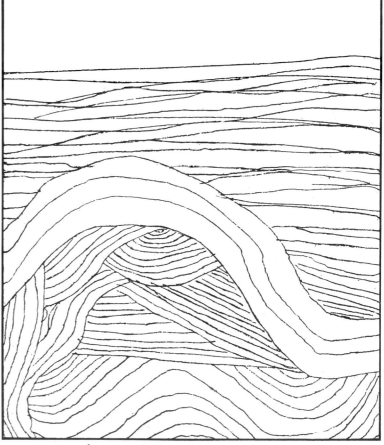

* Notice that REPETITION is the key-note to these designs.   YEAR 6

pencil

LINEAR DESIGNS

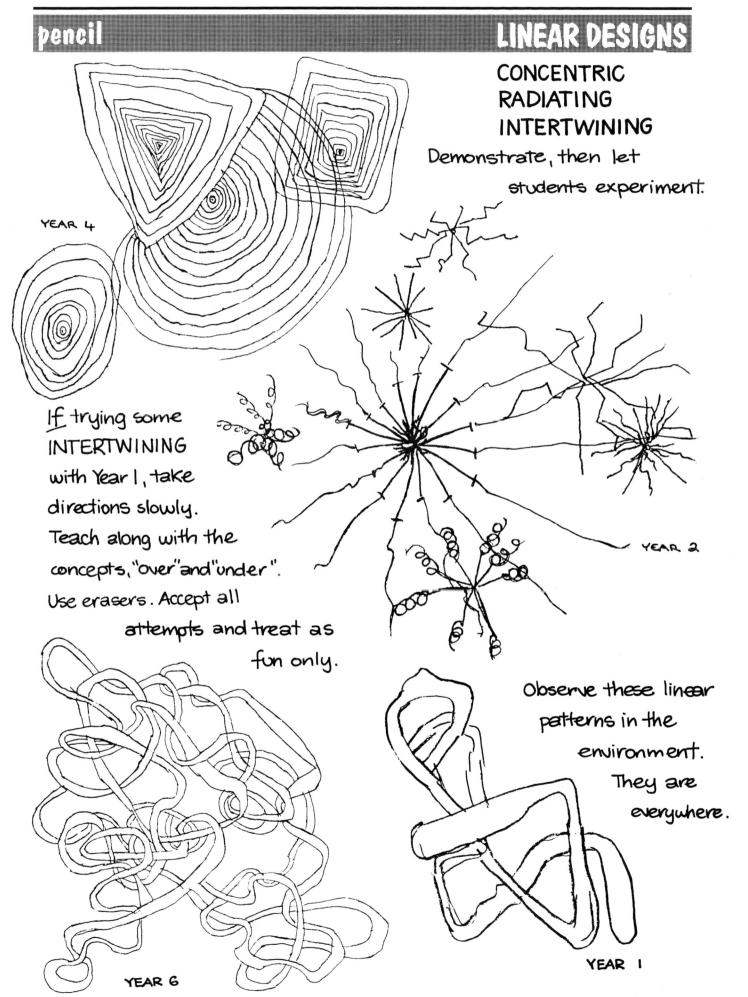

CONCENTRIC
RADIATING
INTERTWINING

Demonstrate, then let
students experiment.

YEAR 4

If trying some
INTERTWINING
with Year 1, take
directions slowly.
Teach along with the
concepts, "over" and "under".
Use erasers. Accept all
attempts and treat as
fun only.

YEAR 2

Observe these linear
patterns in the
environment.
They are
everywhere.

YEAR 6

YEAR 1

LINEAR DESIGNS · DESIGNING   pencil

◀ SPIRALS

YEAR 1

31 designing

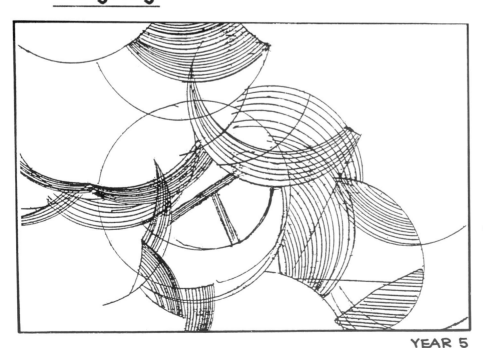

YEAR 5

Designing by children has been greatly underestimated in the past, so be ready for surprises.

[See p. 66 for helpful "directives" given for the designing at left.]

This design, based on the cross-section of an onion, illustrates the child's ability to apply concepts of design learned in Activity 30, pp. 56, 57.

pencil   **DESIGNING**

YEAR 6

See also, p.69.

Above, J.F.Balmer has applied the linear designs in Activity 30, to her own name ~ parallel, radiating, spiral, concentric, intertwining are all there.

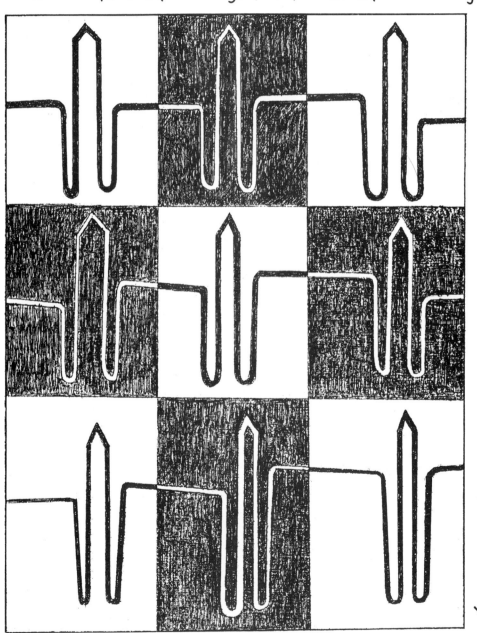

YEAR 7

Above, a teacher works on her own design, with her Year 3 class.

All year levels enjoy these SIMPLE <u>ALL-OVER REPEAT</u> patterns. Younger children need not draw up a NETWORK. Each <u>MOTIF</u> in each <u>UNIT</u> above has been linked. The alternation of motif colour is called <u>COUNTERCHANGE</u>.

AND...

"DOING YOUR OWN thing" TIME

Give... as many oppor-
tunities as possible for
students to select their **own subject**,
their **own media and techniques**
and their **own time limits** ~
perhaps in short sessions over several
days. [It is important that children feel
they have freedom of choice in subject
matter, but if the moral tone of the
subject is questionable, it most certainly
will do no harm to take a "not accept-
able" stance.]

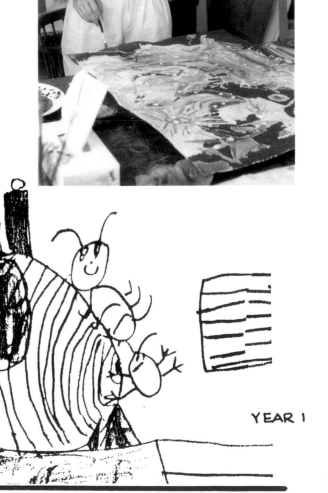

YEAR 1

In this drawing of a pumpkin, note the inclusion of the blackboard writing —
and the one beetle that grew into a whole family ~ the child's own creative input.

SECTION THREE

Evaluation

OBSERVE the student at work ~ to assess confidence, self-reliance, application of knowledge, manipulative skills, work habits, and so on.

"ARE YOU HAPPY WITH WHAT YOU HAVE DONE, ALLISON?"

DOES THE STUDENT NEED HELP?

TALK to the student ~ establish the intentions and compare with results. Was the selection of medium, technique and types of lines, suitable for the subject? Were the intentions directed toward the REALISTIC RECORD, the EXPERI—MENTAL, INTELLECTUAL, IMAGINATIVE, DECORATIVE, AESTHETIC, or as a PERSONAL EXPRESSION ~ or as PRACTICE? See pp. 62-69.

"WHAT IS IT ABOUT, DON?" "WHY DID YOU USE THOSE LINES, HEATHER?"

LOOK at the student's work in relation to all experiences covered so far. Has knowledge been applied? TAKE THE WORK HOME. GIVE IT A GOOD "SEEING" ~ READ IT AS IF IT WAS WRITTEN TO YOU, PERSONALLY. Every mark a student makes means something, so don't miss it.

COMPARE the student's work with previous work. Is he or she trying new things or simply repeating "successful" formulae?

See EVALUATION section in TEACHER'S GUIDE, pp. 57-59.

What to look for—

DON'T FORGET TO TAKE THE STUDENT'S TEMPERAMENT INTO ACCOUNT~ there's the bold and timid, the untidy and meticulous . . . Take care not to react negatively to a type that is opposite to your own. Each style has its own merits and contributions to make. See TEACHER'S GUIDE, pp. 50-55.

REALISTIC RECORD

Sean YEAR 7

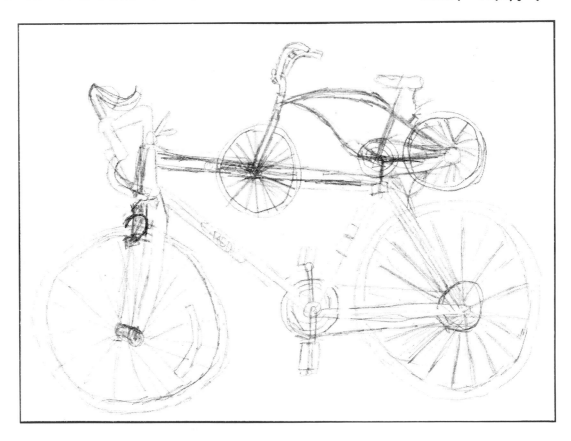

The genuine attempt to depict all the lines in this drawing from life is obvious. The subject is quite complex and the child has achieved a very good presentation of overall proportion as well as detail. Since the objects are of smooth metal, and stream-lined, perhaps his linework could be improved by the practice of smooth, long lines, rather than the typical short, scratchy lines often used for quick sketches. These can become just a habit. [See Activity 19, p. 50.]

Susan
YEAR 1

Elton YEAR 2

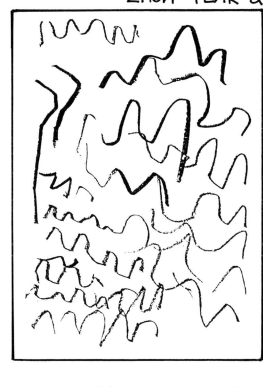

The work on this page shows the
directness of the experimental
approach. Strive to help the students
retain this fresh spontaneity
in their planned work, especially
the older students who
are influenced so much
by peer pressure.

Narelle YEAR 4

Claudine YEAR 7

Debbie YEAR 5

These are four of many quite amazing designs
for seed-pods. These drawings were preceded by
a discussion on Nature's methods of packaging
and dispersal. Repetition was noted in real pods.
The children had to be able to describe how their
designs worked. The pods also had to be pleasing
to the eye. Note the variations and the attractive
use of repetition in each case. Full credit is due
for practicality of design and aesthetics. see
TEACHER'S GUIDE, p.19 ~ "explore scientifically".

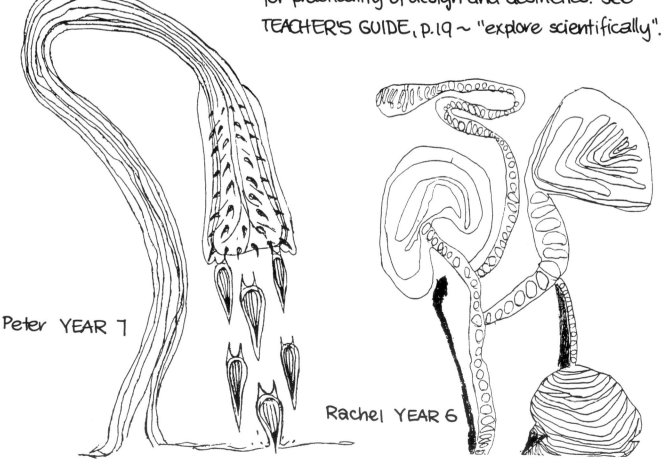

Peter YEAR 7

Rachel YEAR 6

This bold statement of what the child would like if she had one wish shows the power of being able to visualize and put imaginative situations into visual form. Observe the interesting arrangement of lolly-pops and candy sticks in the lower right corner; the overlapping; the decorative repetition of stripes, spirals and concentric circles, encountered in Activity 30, on pp. 56-58; the "saying-it-all" actions of the figure and, most of all, the magic reality of the giant candy stick and lolly-pop. The drawing, produced in quiet concentration, probably says more than the child would have had the opportunity to state verbally to her teacher — a good example of the purpose of drawing as a means of communication.

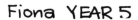
Fiona YEAR 5

DECORATIVE

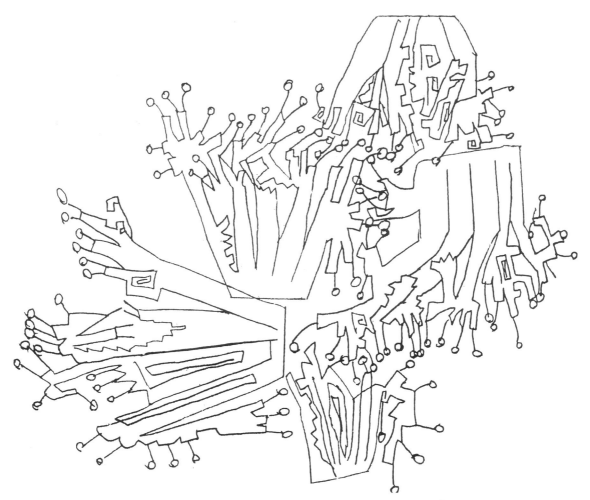

Cameron   YEAR 5

For this design from Activity 31, p.58, the students were given a few simple, general directives: Select one of the supplied cut vegetables [broccoli, onion and cucumber] and draw a shape based on all or any part of the vegetable, using only very straight and/or very smooth curves, in clean line-work. Repeat this shape in any arrangement with the shapes touching and overlapping, so they form one unit. Add any extra lines, omit any lines ~ or shapes. Knowing these directives helps your evaluation of the child's application of them. Note the retention of the complex nature of broccoli, the use of straight-sided spirals encountered during Activity 30, p.58, and the degree of concentration and the perseverance required for the complexity of the whole piece. Having produced such a pleasing design, the child is likely to apply the direct-ives himself in the future, in his own way, in his own context.

The chief delight for the teacher in this work was that it showed that the child had applied, during his own "doing your own thing" time, basic line patterns practised in Activity 30, pp. 56, 57 ~ concentric and parallel lines. He had also balanced the composition well [compare with objects on a see-saw] and linked motifs to give better unity. Compared with his previous design work which was puny and hesitant, this work is a breakthrough. He needs to be watched now, so that he keeps extending his design ideas, and doesn't become repetitive. He obviously gains aesthetic pleasure from design work and could be further encouraged in this area. See notes on Report Cards, TEACHER'S GUIDE, p. 59.

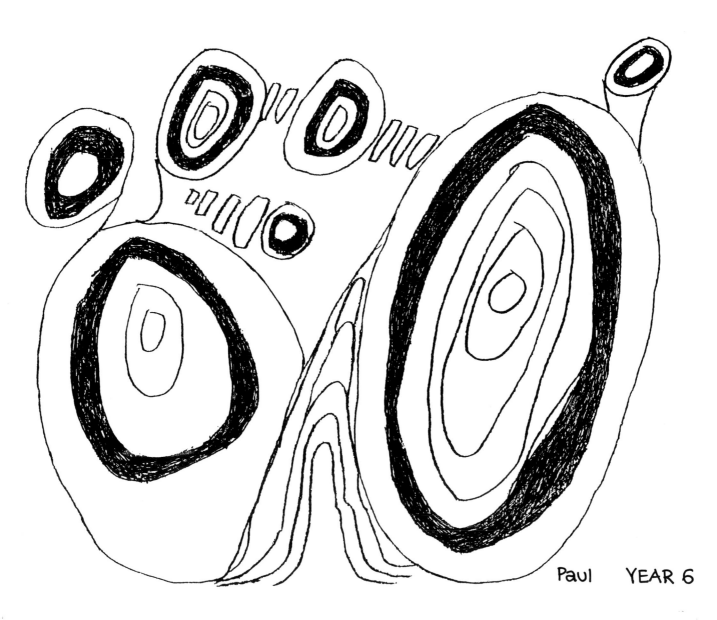

Paul   YEAR 6

PERSONAL EXPRESSION

In these drawings, the children were asked to remember some feeling that was important to them ~ happiness, excitement, fear... The drawing on the right depicts the loss of a balloon. Note how the one balloon is multiplied and all the lines escape upwards, calmly, but inevitably. Below, observe the child's feeling for the energy of the sky~ turbulant clouds, rain, lumps of hail, full force sun ~ with happy children under flower umbrellas.

Craig YEAR 5

Ben YEAR 1

Tony YEAR 6

Imagine the concentration required for the drawing above, joining parallel, intertwining, spiralling, concentric and radiating lines into one unit. The child can obviously manage all those pattern types. His linework may be a little wobbly but his achievement in concentrated effort is worthy of enthusiastic praise. He may enjoy smoothing out the ragged curves into typical "design lines" that flow cleanly and rhythmically.

Practice sessions are important as they provide the opportunity for students to develop skills and ideas initiated in lesson times. Quite often, students reach a high level of skill without any further assistance from the teacher. It is worthwhile organizing these **Daily Drawing** times. It only requires having paper on hand ~ computer paper will do ~ perhaps stapled together as the students' own books. The sessions need not be time-tabled ~just any time the class, or student, is not involved in any other activity. These could last from 2 to 20 minutes or more. They are also handy for calming a class ~ and as a respite for the teacher.

Long live the line!

Here we see students involved with line experiences ~ handling curved line drawing tangled line, moving with a living spiral, discussing their line collection, experimenting with pencil line, tying up trees with line . . .

Long live the line!

. . . drawing line from life, checking out vocabulary, taking line on an adventure, making line dance, and drawing line to music. The photographs show that an Art lesson isn't just about making something from Art materials. It is about the **life** around us ~ *and being in it!*

. . . all ages, all stages.

Shape

Shape

There is a space between awakedness and sleep when shapes appear and pass in strange and orderless procession. Look there! Beyond the vastness of the flat and empty sea, the sun hangs large and low in endless peace. And here, confetti drifts between the deep and rounded caverns of the mind, where harlequins in sequined suits are juggling decks of cards beside the door that opens into dreaming.

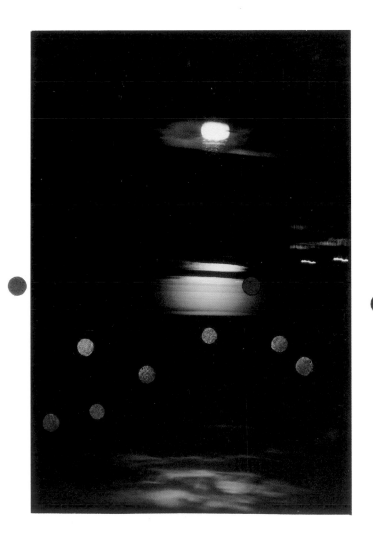

Contents

SUGGESTED WORK PLAN FOR A BLOCK UNIT OF 10 WEEKS ON SHAPE

Mix'n'match your own activities if not using the plan below. Be flexible!
Omit or extend activities where desired or practical. See N.B. LINE, p.5.

WEEK ONE

AWARENESS: Handling shape – ACTIVITY 1...pp.8-11. Vocabulary brainstorming

Seeing shape – ACTIVITY 2...p.12. Seeing safari

PRACTICAL: Other media – ACTIVITY 34...p.53. Coloured-paper collage

OR ACTIVITY 30/31/32/33...pp.52-53. Collage

Start collecting boxes and construction materials for Activity 18-19, WEEK 4, 5.

WEEK TWO

AWARENESS: Seeing shape – ACTIVITY 3...pp.13-15. Audio-visuals. Display

PRACTICAL: Other media – ACTIVITY 22-23...pp.48-49. Clay modelling

WEEK THREE

AWARENESS: Seeing shape – ACTIVITY 7...pp.20-21. Shape display

ACTIVITY 8...p.p.22-23. Recording from life

PRACTICAL: Other media – ACTIVITY 44...p.61. Charcoal frottage

ACTIVITY 21...p.47. Adhesive paper collage

WEEK FOUR

Investigate the possibility of a Gallery excursion for around WEEK 8.

AWARENESS: Seeing shape – ACTIVITY 4...p.16. Appreciation. Student's Book

PRACTICAL: Research – ACTIVITY 17...p.36. Drawing. Collect

Experimental "play" – ACTIVITY 18...pp.37-41. Box City construction

WEEK FIVE

AWARENESS: Integration – ACTIVITY 13...p.29. Writing about shape

PRACTICAL: Directed experience – ACTIVITY 19...pp.42-44. Construction

Applied experience – ACTIVITY 20...pp.45-46. Designing. Compare

with drawings, Activity 17.

The use of **Daily Drawing Books** has proven highly successful. They provide the children with their own "space" in which to develop their own ideas and skills. See LINE, p.69; COLOUR, p.7; TONE, pp.42, 44.

WEEK SIX

<u>AWARENESS</u>:	Integration	— ACTIVITY 9·10...pp.24·25. Drama and Movement. Shadow play
<u>PRACTICAL</u>:	Other media	— ACTIVITY 24·25...p.50. Construction

WEEK SEVEN

<u>AWARENESS</u>:	Integration	— ACTIVITY 12...p.28. Shape with sound
		ACTIVITY 11...pp.26·27. Video shoot
<u>PRACTICAL</u>:	Other media	— ACTIVITY 26·27·28·29...p.51. Masks, kites, Papier maché, Mobiles. Select.

WEEK EIGHT

<u>AWARENESS</u>:	Seeing shape	— ACTIVITY 6...pp.18·19. Appreciation. Student's Book
		ACTIVITY 5...p.17. Gallery visit?
<u>PRACTICAL</u>:		ACTIVITY 43...pp.58-60. Painting

WEEK NINE

<u>AWARENESS</u>:	Integration	— ACTIVITY 14...p.30. Photocopying
		ACTIVITY 15...p.31. Computer graphics
	Language of shape	— ACTIVITY 16...pp.32·33. Word display
<u>PRACTICAL</u>:	Other media	— ACTIVITY 35...p.54. Collage. Spatial relationships
		ACTIVITY 36·37...p.54. Collage. Positive and negative shapes

WEEK TEN

	Other media	— ACTIVITY 38...p.55. Drawing from life. Pencil
		ACTIVITY 39...p.56. Drawing
		ACTIVITY 40...p.57. Thumb prints
		ACTIVITY 41·42...p.57. Stencil. Template
		ACTIVITY 45...p.62. "Doing your own thing" time

<u>N.B.</u> Remember that the above Work Plan is a suggested one only. The whole Program is designed to be flexible, so some activities can be omitted, adapted or extended. What <u>is</u> important is that **AWARENESS EXPERIENCES** are to work hand in hand with **PRACTICAL EXPERIENCES** <u>so that students have a source for their ideas.</u> Also, the build-up of **VOCABULARY** is important for aesthetic development, and **DRAWING FROM LIFE** essential for learning to "see".

Materials

THE BASIC KIT ~ double if possible

CHROMACRYL PAINT — all five colours*... p.p. 51·57·58–60

CLAY — 1½ blocks - 38 kg terra cotta ... p.p. 26·48·49

COLOURED PAPER — 1 pkt matt squares - 254²mm - 360 sh ... pp. 47·50·52–54

GLUE – [powdered] ⟶ 2 litres ... p.p. 47·50–54

Also, if possible —

CHARCOAL – 3 boxes, block ... pp. 59·61

CRAYPAS – 10 boxes ... p. 60

PASTELS – 4 boxes ... pp. 59·60

INK – 1 btle black ... pp. 59·60

THE BARE BONES KIT

CHROMACRYL PAINT — all five colours*... p.p. 51·57·58–60

CLAY — 1 block – 25 kg terra cotta ... p.p. 26·48·49

COLOURED PAPER — 1 pkt matt squares - 254²mm ... pp. 47·50·52–54

SCAVENGE AND SAVE ~ craypas, pastel, ink ... pp. 59·60

MAKE YOUR OWN ~ FLOUR and WATER GLUE ... pp. 47·50–54

CHARCOAL from burnt wood ... pp. 59·61

THE *running on* .... THIN AIR KIT

CHROMACRYL PAINT ~ RED, BLUE, YELLOW*... pp. 51·57·58–60

SCAVENGE AND SAVE, OR MAKE YOUR OWN AS FOR KIT ABOVE

N.B. Teachers with expertise in ceramics may require specific materials.

FOR ALL KITS:
- Collection of "shapes" – seed pods, bones, stones, pottery, instruments, etc. pp. 8–10·20
- Boxes ~ a variety of sizes, dozens to hundreds ... pp. 37–41
- Construction bits and pieces ~ blocks, tubes, plastic containers food cartons, etc. ... pp. 42–44

* Commercial names: Cool Yellow, Warm Red, Warm Blue, Black, White.

SECTION ONE

Awareness experiences

AIMS:
- to awaken an interest in shape **for its own sake**
- to develop a **vocabulary** about shape at all levels of awareness ~ physical to abstract

- HANDLING SHAPE
- SEEING SHAPE
- INTEGRATED EXPERIENCE WITH SHAPE
- LANGUAGE OF SHAPE

RESOURCES

This activity is simple and yet at the very heart of artistic development. Seeing an object as a SHAPE, is a step forward for a start. Then it requires the students to be aware of the attributes of an object beyond its mere physical purpose. These attributes are describable as adjectives or phrases. The activity involves the collection of these words and phrases, to be put onto WORD CARDS at a later date. See pp. 32, 33.

RESOURCES : A **COLLECTION** of objects with as great a variety of shapes as possible. ~

Try to include all the **physical types.** See p.11. If possible, obtain some extreme examples of these, e.g. an <u>enormous</u> shape [a palm frond] and a <u>minute</u> shape [lady beetle]; a very <u>simple</u> shape [a coin] and a very <u>complicated</u> shape [spider shell].

Ensure some objects are from the **students' own environment** ~ toys, sporting gear, clothing, hobby objects ~ fans, kites, boomerangs. **Include other cultures.**

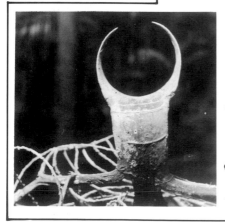

Try to find at least one **mysterious** or huge, **outlandish** shape ~ as an attention-grabber and conversation-starter. Scavenge around in second-hand shops, in the bush, old car yards, the backs of cupboards, or under your elderly aunt's house ~ an old coffee pot? a miner's head lamp? a mandolin? a tuba? an old iron? a gramophone speaker? Quite often this activity will spark off an interest in collections of all sorts and shapes.

VOCABULARY BRAINSTORMING

Students can sit in a circle. Pass the shapes around. Keep awareness on the <u>SHAPE</u>, not what the object is. Start words rolling.

BRAINSTORM!

Ask, "What sort of shape is it? How does it move? What does it feel like? Does it remind you of something?"

"It's flexible."

"...floppy"

"It would make a good wobble-board."

"...it's like a bird's nest."

"It's rigid, but only down the centre."

"It's smooth... and weird."

"It's decorative."

"...rough and hollow"

"It's like a gum-nut."

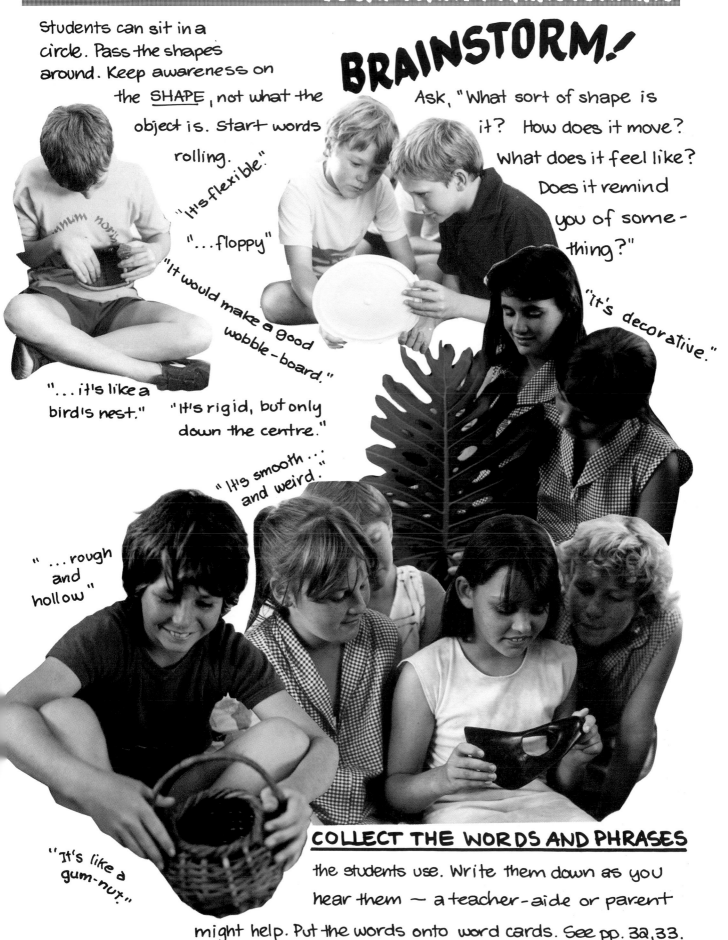

COLLECT THE WORDS AND PHRASES

the students use. Write them down as you hear them — a teacher-aide or parent might help. Put the words onto word cards. See pp. 32,33.

VOCABULARY BRAINSTORMING

handy hints

IT IS IMPORTANT THAT THE STUDENTS **ENJOY** THIS FIRST, DIRECTED EN-
COUNTER WITH YOU AND SHAPE. <u>SO,</u> **SACRIFICE** YOUR ATTENTION TO
WRITING DOWN THE WORDS THEY USE IF IT MEANS KEEPING RELAXED AND
ENJOYING IT YOURSELF. USUALLY, WORDS COME SLOWLY THEN START TO SNOW-
BALL. REMEMBER, THE AIM IS TO ESTABLISH <u>AWARENESS OF SHAPES</u> AND
TO <u>USE WORDS</u> TO DESCRIBE THEM. COLLECT AS MANY AS YOU CAN.

Tell the students you are collecting their words and phrases.

Ensure every student contributes words or phrases if possible.

If the class is large, over-responsive, or difficult to manage,
consider workable strategies, e.g.
Teacher holds up objects one by one, for discussion, establishing an
orderly sequence of . . . 1. discussion of object with class

Photograph: John Turnock, Qld Department of Education

       2. eliciting descriptive words
       3. time taken by teacher to write down
          words offered by students
       4. some free talk about the object
The activity could be arranged as part of
contract work for middle and upper year levels.
Students can work in groups or individually,
at tables with objects on them, adding to a list,
or making their own list of words and phrases
describing the shapes. The teacher would need
to start the ball rolling. A dictionary and
Roget's Thesaurus would be useful. Occasional
checking of the list is recommended. see p. 33.

PHYSICAL TYPES OF SHAPE

All shapes can be described according to **abstract** qualities they are seen to posess by the viewer, e.g. stolid, festive. The shapes below are described according to their **physical** attributes only.

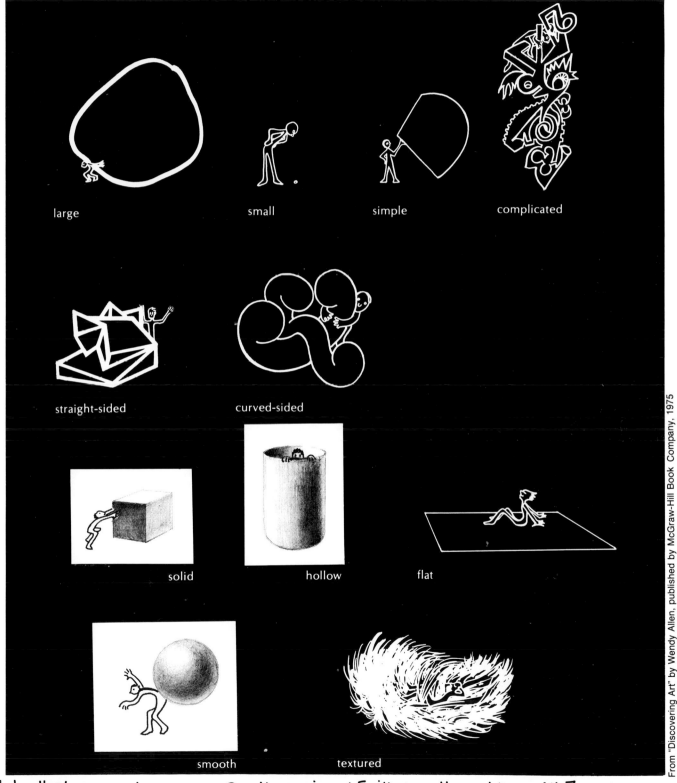

large   small   simple   complicated

straight-sided   curved-sided

solid   hollow   flat

smooth   textured

From "Discovering Art" by Wendy Allen, published by McGraw-Hill Book Company, 1975

Note that some shapes are 2-dimensional [with length and breadth] and some are 3-dimensional [with length, breadth, and depth].

THE SEEING SAFARI

AIMS:
- to help the students learn to 'SEE', ie. to see **more** than the mere physical presence of objects
- to develop further a **VOCABULARY** about shape on all levels of awareness ~ physical to abstract

Take the class on a search for interesting shapes in the school yard or other appropriate area. Find the physical types set out on p.11, then discuss other characteristics. Which is the heaviest, the noisiest, the most dangerous, the ugliest, and so on.

Have you brought your camera? Any tape in the video camera?

RAINING? Take an indoor safari, or play a quick game of "I SPY" in the classroom ... hollow shape? a long, flat, pointed shape? a curved and straight-sided shape? a shape like the prow of a Viking ship? a circular shape like a U.F.O.? a lively shape? a crazy, "whoopie!" shape?

Before going on safari, it is best to check out the proposed trail. Prepare a few new words ~ "discover" them and add them to the class list,

e.g. **BEDRAGGLED** [crumpled rag, dead flower]

STUBBORN [post, door-stopper]

See list, p.33, and keep Roget's Thesaurus close by, if you have one.

MAKING THE MOST OF MEDIA

AUDIO-VISUAL RESOURCES:

Use an overhead projector creatively. In a shallow glass dish, mix water and a little detergent. Add a small amount of turpentine and a few blobs of cooking oil. Experiment with amounts. Fascinating reactions should work for hours. Colour with food colouring.

Investigate sources of videos, films, strips, etc. about SHAPE, and/or make some yourself. Ask school and community Libraries, Education Centres, Film Centres, and so on.

Check the school television and radio broadcasts for Art programs. Timetables are usually available at the beginning of each year. Try to build up the school's resources as well as your own.

WATCH AND DISCUSS.

STATIC RESOURCES:

LOOK AND DISCUSS.

See next page.

DISPLAY in the classroom, or elsewhere in the school ~

- photographs you, or others, have taken
- pictures from magazines
- newspaper photographs
- posters
- record covers, book covers, and so on.

You may have space for only **ONE** photograph in your classroom ~ fine!

It will have unrivalled status of importance ~ but do change it often.

MEDIA classroom display

SHAPES OF NATURE

WEATHERED ROCK — enormous, solid ... like an abandoned dog's bone

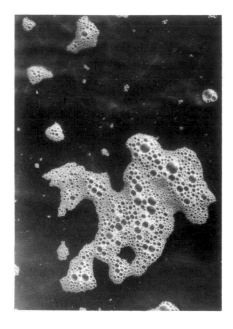

FROTH AND BUBBLE OF THE SEA — interesting ... like a map

CLASSROOM DISPLAY

CLOUDS — ever-changing, elusive, silent shapes ... like ghosts

PLANT FORMS — bristling blobs with radiating serrated arms ... like octopi

classroom display

SHAPES OF OUR OWN!

Displays lend themselves easily to **THEMES** and could be based on objects from the children's own interests and hobbies. Posters of shells, model boats, photographs of students fishing, and so on, could create a theme of SHAPES OF THE SEA. Add photographs from magazines.

As well as guiding students to appreciate shapes in Nature and the adult world, help them to appreciate the special qualities of objects in their own world. Have a "Bring Your Own Shape" Day. [You'd better exclude anything that barks, bites, or will escape!] Include objects belonging to the children in the shape displays. The owners can write their own captions or descriptive words. All this helps engender awareness of cultural heritage ~ pride in one's own "traditions", tolerance of those of others. Younger children will enjoy a teddy bears' picnic. Take photographs to add to the display.

APPRECIATION IN THE WORLD OF ART

Try to build up your own and the school's resources. Cover different Art forms — painting, drawing, printing, sculpture, architecture, ceramics, textiles, etc. Look for good examples showing the artists' use of physical types of shapes, e.g. flat, hollow, curve-sided, and discuss how they have been arranged expressively ~ like dancing pyramids, sails, patch-work . . .

DISCUSS the Art works below in conjunction with the Student's Book, pp. 7, 10 and 13.

Courtesy of the National Gallery of Victoria

"DEATH IN A GARDEN" by Leonard FRENCH [b. 1928 AUST.]. Enamel on hessian-covered hardboard. Note geometry of the shapes.

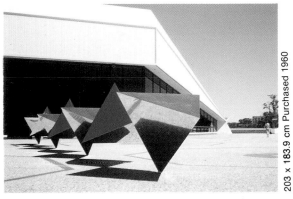

203 × 183.9 cm Purchased 1960

Sculpture by Bert FLUGELMAN [b. 1923 AUSTRIA]. Set of stainless steel pyramids, Adelaide Festival Theatre, S.A.

Photograph: Len Shillam, Queensland

Sydney Opera House, N.S.W. Architect: Joern UTZON.

Expo '88, Brisbane

Indian totem pole outside Canadian pavilion, Brisbane, Expo 88. Symmetry is a strong feature of all totemic designs.

APPRECIATION IN THE WORLD OF ART

visiting a Gallery
... make it a happy occasion!

- Ensure your Gallery visits are purposeful. Plan ahead so you can relax at the Gallery. Use the visit as an exciting way to introduce, develop or consolidate work you are doing in the classroom.

- Contact the Gallery several weeks before you intend to visit, irrespective of how small the Gallery is. Most large Galleries have an Educational Section and trained officers will conduct the students on a tour. Discuss what you have been doing in your Art Program so that the officer, or Gallery Director if available, can relate this to the content of the talk to the students.

Students at the Queensland Art Gallery.

- Do work sheets, questionnaires, and so on, back at school. Let the students spend their Gallery time looking to see what others are trying to tell them. Relate it to their own work where possible. Artists are people with something to say, just like them.

- Keep any problem students happily busy. Ask them to act out the pose of a sculpture, or describe what is happening in a painting. Let them feel a Gallery is a hospitable place for them.

- Encourage the students and their parents to visit Galleries out of school time. Take as many parents as possible on the visit. Often, it is their first visit and it breaks down a barrier of "cultural cringe".

- Enjoy the day! It is important to form positive attitudes and happy memories to carry into the future.

APPRECIATION   discussing our differences

EVERYONE IS DIFFERENT! WE ALL APPRECIATE THINGS DIFFERENTLY!
LET'S TALK ABOUT IT. See STUDENT'S BOOK, P.2.

TAKE, FOR INSTANCE, <u>**PAINTINGS**</u> ~

Display several large reproductions, or originals if possible, of different styles, e.g. realistic, semi-abstract and abstract. Ask children's opinions of each. Emphasize that, because we have all had different experiences in life, of course we have different opinions. No-one is "wrong" or "right" ~ just different. In the paintings at left, by the author, although they are all "landscapes" with rocks and water, each is in a different style. The top one is **realistic**, like a photograph. The middle one is **semi-abstract** and about patterns of erosion. The bottom one, an **abstract**, is about the design of rippling water and tumbling rocks. Discuss these paintings with the students using the Student's Book, p.2.

Opposite, are buildings from different cultural backgrounds. What is normal for some people is different for others. Belonging is important, but let's share the interesting differences!

APPRECIATION IN THE WORLD AROUND US

See STUDENT'S BOOK, p.12.

<u>SHOPS AND CHURCHES</u> — what are their shapes in your neighbourhood?

What do the shapes of these buildings tell us about the people who use them?

How do the designs suit the purpose for which they were built?
What shape building would you design for a shop or church?

MAKING A SHAPE DISPLAY

SHAPES ON CENTRE STAGE

REMEMBER ... LABELS are IMPORTANT!!!
~ the students can write these themselves

No room for display ?...The shapes could be collected in a box and brought out for short discussion sessions or morning talks. They could be used for still-life drawing groups. They could be subject starters for stories, for creative writing...

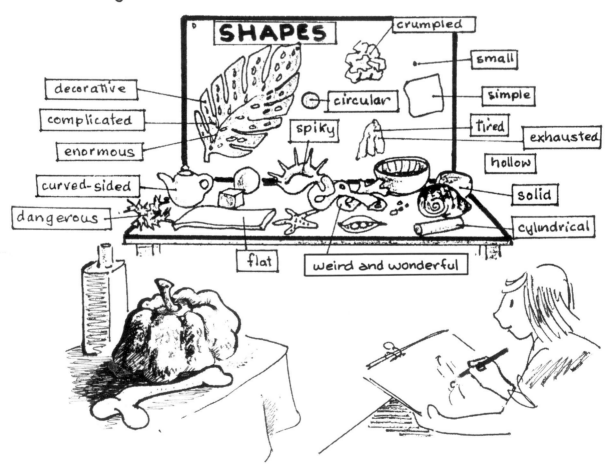

COLLECTIONS SUCH AS THESE CAN CONTINUE ALL YEAR AND HAVE MANY USES, ESPECIALLY IN SCIENCE LESSONS.

MAKING A SHAPE DISPLAY

The drawings below are from Year One, top row, and Year Five, bottom row. All are based on Monstera leaves in classroom displays. Add drawings from other year levels to your own displays. Discuss different approaches.

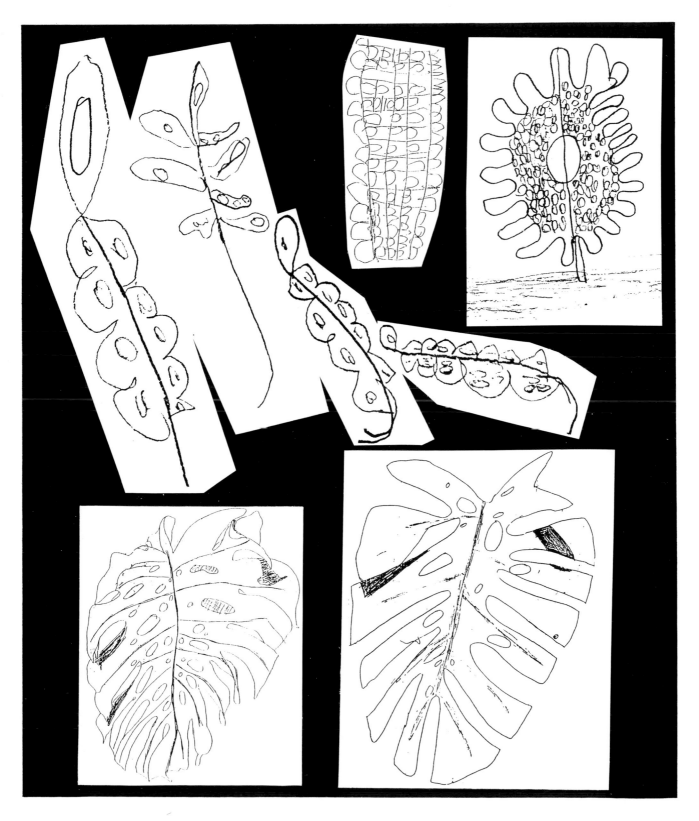

RECORDING SHAPES FROM LIFE

See TEACHER'S GUIDE, pp. 22-27.

The easiest and most valuable lesson of all!

Take pencils and paper out into the school-yard. Draw as great a variety of shapes as time allows ~ 15 to 30 minutes? Before setting out, briefly discuss different types of shapes ~ hollow, flat, solid, etc. and those with character or feeling ~ fragile, lazy, hostile, etc. Emphasize drawing JUST SHAPES, not a picture or drawing of an object. See follow-up lesson, p.69.

Don't forget the camera. Take the opportunity to build up resources.

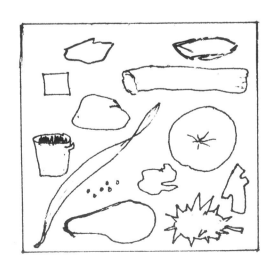

◀ A student's page might look like this.

DISPLAY all the students' work if possible. Otherwise make a selection. A heading?

WHAT AM I ?

RECORDING SHAPES FROM LIFE

think of new ideas

INSTEAD OF JUST LOOKING FOR <u>ANY</u> INTERESTING SHAPE, FIND —

- hollow shapes that make good sounds when tapped with a pencil
- straight-sided shapes that have more than four corners
- the man-made shape that is newest to the environment
- any shape that can be found in different sizes
- flat shapes only large enough to hold a dozen ants
- any shape that tapers at one end
- curved-sided shapes that could be rolled down a hill if not attached to anything else
- any shape that is used to hold something together. [This idea has been used by a professional artist for a whole exhibition of paper constructions. The students might like to develop their ideas also.]

<u>Then</u>, as a follow-up, see the sculpture design on p. 38 of the TEACHER'S GUIDE.

<u>Also</u>, since the students themselves are part of the environment, they can draw each other. Make a class portrait show. See p. 34 of the TEACHER'S GUIDE.

YEAR 1

YEAR 7

USING SHAPE IN DRAMA

❋ let's move

For thousands of years people have communicated through body movement.
In the classroom, let's look at it this way ~

- when <u>reading</u> or <u>hearing</u> the word "sway" students are no better
  off in understanding what it is

- when <u>watching</u> something or someone sway, students have a better
  chance of understanding

- but when students <u>sway themselves</u> they have had to put brain
  and muscle into appropriate action, and they are best able to
  understand the word and experience its character ~ they also
  GATHER ASSOCIATIONS WHICH ARE UNIQUE TO THEMSELVES !

Put all the above three together and, surely, we have done our best. We also
have <u>VISUAL EVIDENCE</u> of the students' understanding. We now know it
is in their "repertoires" to use in their own creativity, if desired.

<u>So</u> ~ let's go !

As individuals, be a ... swaying shape, stubborn shape,
tense shape ...

As groups, be a ... large shape, hollow shape ...

As groups, be ... a lazy shape [like melting butter], an
excited shape [like a happy octopus] ...

<u>N.B.</u>

See p. 33
for types of
shapes.

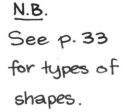

lazy,
tired,
languid
shape

active,
excited,
jubilant
shape

WATCHING SHAPE

✳ fun with shadow plays

Requirements
{
1 overhead projector
1 broom [or similar long stick]
2 students [to hold up broom]
1 sheet [pinned over broom]
}

FOR YOUR OWN "T.V. STATION"!!

a. Students use themselves as . . . JUMPING shapes, JERKY shapes, OOZING shapes, FRENZIED shapes, SWOONING shapes, SLOTH-LIKE shapes. . .

Audience's view with students between screen and projector.

b. Students cut out cardboard shapes and attach them to wire holders [coat hangers] and hold these against the sheet at the back. Write and direct plays about SHAPES [rather than objects or people].

c. **MOST EXCITING OF ALL...**
Place objects or cut-outs down on horizontal top of the projector. Place cellophane on top for colour. EXPERIMENT with anything transparent, eg. water in a glass.

d. **TRY SOME STORY-TELLING**
"Once upon a time, there was a ghostly shape called SPOOKLES, and a square called SQUAWK, and his brothers, SQUEEK and SQUICK. One dark, stormy night......"

WATCHING SHAPE

❋ bring out the video camera

a) TRY SOME DISAPPEARING TRICKS WITH SHAPE

Can you turn a student into another shape ~ and another, and another ?

5 SECONDS ↑ 4 SECONDS ↑ 2 SECONDS ↑ 4 SECONDS ↑ 4 SECONDS ↑ 4 SECONDS ↑ 4 SECONDS ↑
    CUT   CUT   CUT   CUT   CUT   CUT

and so on...

Add interesting sound effects and/or "voice over".

b) TRY SOME ANIMATION ~ with a lump of clay

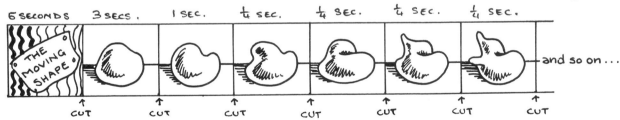

5 SECONDS   3 SECS.   1 SEC. $\frac{1}{2}$ SEC. $\frac{1}{4}$ SEC. $\frac{1}{4}$ SEC. $\frac{1}{4}$ SEC.

↑ CUT   ↑ CUT   ↑ CUT   ↑ CUT   ↑ CUT   ↑ CUT   ↑ CUT

and so on...

- Keep camera perfectly still on tripod throughout.
- Keep base of clay in same position throughout.
- You will need to change the shape of the clay about 100 times for only a half a minute of viewing ... So, PATIENCE is needed.
- change the shape only slightly each time, so it isn't _too_ jumpy.

c) MAKE YOUR OWN SHAPE RESOURCES ~

- Video objects from your SHAPE COLLECTION for Activity 7, p.20.
- Video shapes around the school - attach wordcards to describe them.
- Video interesting shapes in the community environment.
- Video _any_ of the activities or practical work in this Unit.

WATCHING SHAPE

✳ be creative with the video camera

SHAPES FROM DIFFERENT ETHNIC GROUPS

- Ask students to collect objects characteristic of different ethnic groups ~ hats, shoes, ornaments, etc. Plan your video so that the cultures represented are identified with headings or captions. Add maps, flags, photographs ~ and of course, the students themselves. Develop ideas about the shapes.

DRAMATISE A STORY ABOUT A SHAPE

- Find a story about an object [or two], e.g. a teapot or hat, that would lend itself to dramatization ~ or write one yourself. Give most attention during the video-ing to the object ~ changing the light, the position of viewing, zooming in and out, using close-ups, and so on. The aim of the exercise is to give the students experience in more in-depth appreciation of a single, ordinary object. Bestowing such status upon something quite mundane in our environment is common to artists, e.g. Van Gogh's bedroom chair.

USING SHAPE WITH MUSIC

❋ let's look and listen

N.B. Conceiving shape in terms of sound is not always easy, so let's not push the point. However, if you wish to listen and feel shape in music, try "Aragonaise" by Massenet, or the opening passages of Bach's "Toccata and Fugue in D Minor".

LET'S PUT <u>SOUND</u> AND <u>SHAPES WE CAN SEE</u> TOGETHER ～

- **BECOME UNIDENTIFIED OBJECTS** ～

Photograph: Mark Ross, Queensland

Paint some old sheets and form unusual shapes. Now select some SUITABLE eerie or "unearthly" music to accompany their movement. Try some of Bartok's or Stravinsky's music.

- **BE A HUMAN WASHING LINE** ～ Hang out the tea towels, a sheet or parachute cloth. Flap in the wind. Spotlight in a dark room?

Sway to "Barcarolle" by Offenbach, "Ballet of the Sylphs" by Berlioz, or try some Hawaiian guitar music. Speed it up to some very fast, energetic music of the students' own choice.

SEE HOW RECTANGLES CAN CONVULSE, FLAP, SWAY, FLOAT, RIPPLE, FLOP, VIBRATE...

WHO SAID A RECTANGLE WAS DULL!?!

N.B. See TEXTURE, p. 48, re source of suggested music pieces.

✳ writing about shape

Here are some **visualizing** experiences to precede the writing.
Students close their eyes and see images in their "minds' eyes" ～

" Imagine the following as if it was all on the T.V. screen.
<u>Close your eyes</u> . . .

a) Look up high above you. There's a shape larger than anything else you have ever seen before. It's growing larger and larger. Quick! Slide down this long, dark, tunnel. Here we go!

b) There is a circle right in front of your eyes. See it as a clock face, the sun, a coin, a yawn, looking down on top of a bald head . . . What else could it be?

c) Pretend to hold a piece of clay. Flatten it on top, push a hole right through the middle, squash it flat, then blow it up until it bursts! "

- Now, who can write a **poem** about shapes?
- Who can write about space, or spaces [negative shapes — "where no shape is"], in a short **prose piece**?
- Who can put words collected so far [see p. 33] into a **story**, perhaps about shapes from another planet ～ around the class, a sentence from everyone, writing?
- Who can write a **riddle**? WHAT AM I? Describe shape only.

MAKING USE OF TECHNOLOGY   photocopier

❋ creating with the photocopier

a) Photocopy two or more photographs. Cut out parts of one photocopy and glue onto the whole one. This way, mice can lift mountains, Aunty Barb can kiss frogs, and we can all go **running on rainbows!**

b) Arrange any flat objects on the photocopier — combs, handkerchiefs, tickets, leaves, etc. Try a dark coloured or patterned cloth on top. Use for SHAPE displays. see p. 20.

c) Make multiple copies of a drawn shape, cut them out and glue into an interesting arrangement. See TEACHER'S GUIDE, p. 42 and illustration at left.

d) Experiment by moving drawings, paintings, objects, photographs, etc. while the machine is photocopying. The effects can be quite eerie!

Aunty Barb kisses a frog.

A class of children are using photocopy machines creatively at the Pompidou Cultural Centre, Paris — behind glass so that the public can watch. "Collages" are being made with no pasting involved.

computer | MAKING USE OF TECHNOLOGY

✳ fun with computer graphics

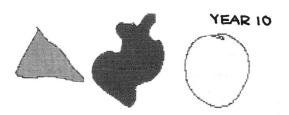

YEAR 10

Computers lend themselves admirably to the exploration of **composition**. By moving certain shapes around, students can see in which position they look best. See TEACHER'S GUIDE, p.35. See the Principles of Composition in the TEACHER'S GUIDE, pp. 33–49.

Also, try combining image-making with **invention** and **problem-solving**, e.g. starting with an exciting object such as a bicycle built for five people, or a rocket. Students could create an on-going story about the object and how it grows as the inventor adds to or changes its design. Each student could narrate the "problems" of the design, e.g. fallout causing pollution. The next student could change the image to solve the problem. The next child could find another hypothetical design problem, e.g. the wings being too heavy, and so on.

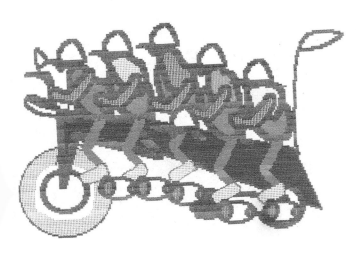

YEAR 7

Another exercise could involve drawing the front of the school, transferring this onto the computer screen, then changing roof shape, stairs, doorways, and so on as if for renovations.

N.B. For producing negative shapes, see TONE, Activity 14, p.20.

COLLECTION AND DISPLAY OF WORDS

COLLECTION AND DISPLAY

✳ This is a ˋBIGˊ MOMENT ～ a tally of the vocabulary that has been collected so far.

LET'S CHECK AND ORGANISE A
READY- REFERENCE BANK
FOR THE FUTURE

Collect all the words and good phrases USED, HEARD or SEEN and add any more you wish from

- your collected list
- a dictionary
- the Art program
- a thesaurus

OR  memory

BEST IDEA...If you haven't already done so, put these words onto WORD CARDS for future resources, displays, and so on.

SEE NEXT PAGE.

Now

DISPLAY ALL THE WORDS AND GOOD PHRASES FOR THE CLASS TO SEE.

COLLECTION AND DISPLAY OF WORDS

some words related to shape

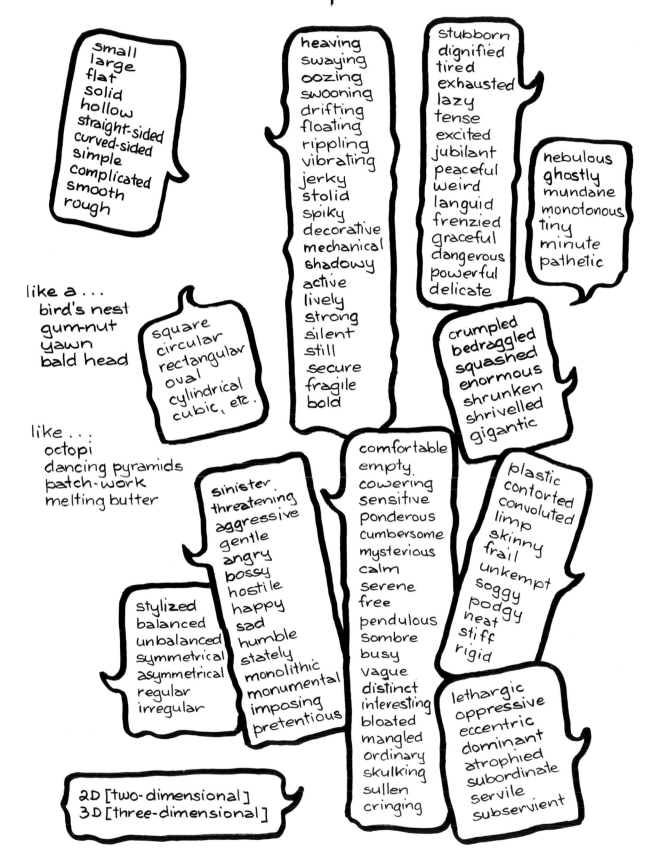

small
large
flat
solid
hollow
straight-sided
curved-sided
simple
complicated
smooth
rough

heaving
swaying
oozing
swooning
drifting
floating
rippling
vibrating
jerky
stolid
spiky
decorative
mechanical
shadowy
active
lively
strong
silent
still
secure
fragile
bold

stubborn
dignified
tired
exhausted
lazy
tense
excited
jubilant
peaceful
weird
languid
frenzied
graceful
dangerous
powerful
delicate

nebulous
ghostly
mundane
monotonous
tiny
minute
pathetic

like a...
bird's nest
gum-nut
yawn
bald head

square
circular
rectangular
oval
cylindrical
cubic, etc.

crumpled
bedraggled
squashed
enormous
shrunken
shrivelled
gigantic

like...
octopi
dancing pyramids
patch-work
melting butter

sinister
threatening
aggressive
gentle
angry
bossy
hostile
happy
sad
humble
stately
monolithic
monumental
imposing
pretentious

comfortable
empty
cowering
sensitive
ponderous
cumbersome
mysterious
calm
serene
free
pendulous
sombre
busy
vague
distinct
interesting
bloated
mangled
ordinary
skulking
sullen
cringing

plastic
contorted
convoluted
limp
skinny
frail
unkempt
soggy
podgy
neat
stiff
rigid

stylized
balanced
unbalanced
symmetrical
asymmetrical
regular
irregular

lethargic
oppressive
eccentric
dominant
atrophied
subordinate
servile
subservient

2D [two-dimensional]
3D [three-dimensional]

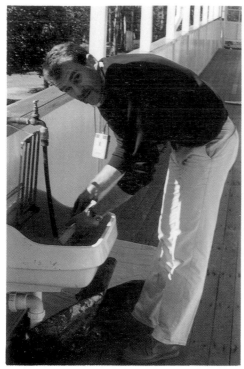

IMPORTANT PEOPLE IN YOUR LIFE

As you can see above, there are other people in the school community who can be of invaluable assistance ~ often to their own delight . . . a voluntary assistant [especially if endowed with Art expertise], a Mum joining in, the cleaner, the janitor, a Dad and an interested Principal.

SECTION TWO
Practical experiences

The shapes around us.

Making our own shapes.

- <u>SOME SIMPLE RESEARCH</u>

- <u>EXPERIENCE IN THE MOST SUITABLE MEDIUM ~ CONSTRUCTION</u>

  - EXPERIMENTAL "PLAY" – construction

  - DIRECTED EXPERIENCE – construction

  - APPLIED EXPERIENCE – drawing

- <u>OTHER MEDIA AND TECHNIQUES</u> : collage; clay modelling ; construction [low relief and free standing ; masks, kites, papier maché, mobiles] ; more collage [separation design, mosaic, fold-and-cut-paper design, cloth and coloured-paper collage — spatial relationships, positive and negative shapes] ; drawing from life ; more drawing ideas ; printing [thumb, stencil and template] ; painting ; frottage

- <u>"DOING YOUR OWN THING" TIME</u>

A SIMPLE EXERCISE

Before doing Activities 18 and 19, try some simple research and assessment. You might like to try it several times during the year to see if the students have developed further or reverted to old habits.

● SIMPLY ASK THE STUDENTS TO DRAW A HOUSE. Give no further directions — just ask for the house they normally draw. Give only a few minutes. Make sure they put their names on them. Collect and compare with drawings you ask them to do, given the same directions and time, <u>AFTER</u> they have done Activities 18 and 19. Go <u>immediately</u> from Activity 19 to the drawing. [Try this even if you don't do Activity 18.]

<u>YOU CAN EXPECT</u> ~ in the first year of using "Running on Rainbows"...

● <u>FIRST DRAWING</u> : the traditional symbolic house, passed down through the family history — with some individual variations ~

● <u>SECOND and SUBSEQUENT DRAWINGS</u> : A new concept at work ... the visualization of actual FORMS making up the construction, in the same way an architect works. <u>OR</u> new concepts added to the old — old habits <u>do</u> die hard !

See pages 45,46

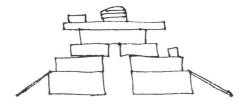

[After several years of "Running on Rainbows"? Move over Le Corbusier!]

the box city activity   EXPERIMENTAL "PLAY"

REQUIREMENTS:

1. Plenty of **INITIATIVE**!
2. Several hundred or so card-board **BOXES**, from refrigerator to match-box size, and any packing materials.

   • Ask at any electrical goods shops, supermarkets, etc.

   • No transport? Delegate the task to parents and class.

   • No storage? Use a corner under the school, or share the collection around several classrooms, ~ OR just <u>have</u> a day of chaos! Teach the children to cope with unusual situations.

Now . . . FIND A BUILDING SITE IN THE SCHOOLGROUND ~ WITH NO WIND!

ASK THE STUDENTS TO BUILD WHATEVER THEY LIKE   LET THEM ORGANIZE THEMSELVES!

Now, take a seat and watch. In 30 minutes you will witness ~ DEMOCRACY, ANARCHY, SOCIALISM, COMMUNISM, COLONISATION, REVOLUTION, CONSPIRACY, ÉLITE-ISM, PACIFICISM . . . and moments of . . . excitement, frustration, greed, anger, submission, boredom, threat, rejection, hilarity, disappointment, apathy, enlightenment, sympathy, determination and triumph. If necessary, venture into the melée, issue a few edicts, and postulate a few policies of the United Nations. Learning to co-operate is a slow process for some! The more practice they have, however, the easier it becomes.

EXPERIMENTAL "PLAY"   the box city activity

Be prepared for some students to play inside the boxes — a natural reaction, especially on the first occasion. Let them enjoy it, then insist on some building. Praise the conscientious builders and let the others hear.

" . . . . we're just getting involved with SHAPE, Sir. "

Keep the end result in mind. See pp. 45, 46.

the box city activity | EXPERIMENTAL "PLAY"

three basic constructions — easily made with boxes

1. POST AND BEAM

The simple Post and Beam construction used at Stonehenge in prehistory days, is still basic to our architecture ~ as in our own houses.

2. The ARCHED DOORWAY

This corbelled style is simple.

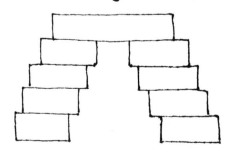

This self-styled arched doorway is decorated with "gargoyles" and "column"

3. CANTILEVER CONSTRUCTION —

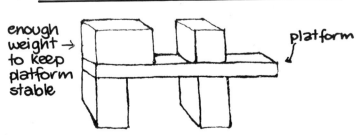

enough weight → to keep platform stable

platform

ENCOURAGE STUDENTS TO LOOK AT ARCHITECTURE BOOKS IN THE LIBRARY.

EXPERIMENTAL "PLAY"   the box city activity

the box city activity   EXPERIMENTAL "PLAY"

a few thoughts about Box City activity

The BOX CITY ACTIVITY is an invaluable introduction to studies involving structure, as in Architecture and Engineering.

- EACH DECISION A STUDENT MAKES IN THE PLACEMENT OF A BOX OR OTHER SHAPE INVOLVES THE **SAME** THOUGHT PROCESSES AS ANY **PROFESSIONAL ARCHITECT** ~ Is the shape going to work here? STRUCTURAL FUNCTION. Will it fall over? STRUCTURAL STABILITY. Is there enough room inside for us? SOCIAL FUNCTION. Does it look good? VISUAL AESTHETICS. Is it a "fantastic", "snazzy" idea? DESIGN ORIGINALITY. And so on.

- EACH ARRANGEMENT A STUDENT MAKES THAT IS RELATIVELY STABLE, WILL PROBABLY INVOLVE A **PROFESSIONAL CONSTRUCTION METHOD** WITH A HISTORY ABLE TO BE FOLLOWED UP IN THE CLASSROOM OR LIBRARY, eg, POST AND LINTEL • the CORBELLED ARCH • the KEY-STONE ARCH • the DOME • the BUTTRESS [including the FLYING BUTTRESS] • CANTILEVERS • SUSPENSION BRIDGING, and so on. See p. 39.

Any student showing a special interest in architectural design can be directed to books on Architecture. See Jason's report, Teacher's Guide, p. 59.

DIRECTED EXPERIENCE   construction

REQUIREMENTS:

1. MORE **INITIATIVE!**

2. A HUNDRED or so _small_ boxes [shoe-box size or smaller], blocks of wood, plastic lids, corrugated and smooth cardboard, stiff plastic, egg cartons, polystyrene trays, and so on. **ANY** materials for construction small enough for an individual at a desk. This is "junk stuff," easily available.

ASK STUDENTS TO CONSTRUCT A BUILDING — with an entrance, rooms, roof, and so on. Encourage some "way-out" designing, i.e. encourage some **divergent** thinking. Accept <u>all</u> designs. Discuss what some designs could be SUITABLE for ~ City Halls, restaurants, castles, churches...

construction   DIRECTED EXPERIENCE

Use the words "ARCHITECTURE" and "ARCHITECT" from Year 1 upwards. Let the students know they are working like the professionals do ~ creating RHYTHM with curved lines, as on the left, using SYMMETRICAL BALANCE, as below, etc. This session might easily be the starting point for a vocational ambition to study architecture in the future, for both girls and boys. The interest, at least, could be a lifetime's.

DIRECTED EXPERIENCE   construction

Architects of the future ?!

For follow-up study, students can look for :

- ancient ziggurats
- Japanese temples
- Frank Lloyd Wright's buildings

- Le Corbusier's buildings
- Gothic cathedrals
- books on modern architecture

Now... ask students to

DESIGN THEIR OWN BUILDING ~ one they would like to have built. It doesn't have to be like the one they just built with blocks, etc. Draw it in pencil. Collect these and compare them with the first drawing. [see page 36]. Photocopy any interesting work and keep for future reference.

All the above drawings are by Year One children, immediately after Activity 19. RATHER THAN TRADITIONAL SYMBOLS, THEY ARE DRAWING FORMS THEY HAVE <u>VISUALIZED</u>! A TREMENDOUS BREAKTHROUGH!...and so easy!

APPLIED EXPERIENCE   *construction designing*

Note how the students are actually "constructing" with "solid forms" on the flat, 2-dimensional page. They are **VISUALIZING** the constructions in the 3-dimensional ~ a far cry from the process required for drawing the traditional symbol for a house. They are now working at a "professional" level. All they need now is knowledge and experience that will come in future years.

YEAR 1

YEAR 1

YEAR 2

YEAR 4

YEAR 5

COLLAGE

YEAR 5

This type of abstract design can be used for catalogue covers, book covers, and so on, or just as design for its own sake.

Black or other coloured Contact* is an excellent medium for cutting out interesting shapes, arranging, and then re-arranging before finally sticking down into pleasing compositions. Ordinary paper shapes will suffice if Contact is not available. For other Collage ideas, see pp. 52-54.

* or other adhesive paper.

CLAY MODELLING

The commercially – made terra-cotta clay is excellent for the classroom situation. It is ready for use, and can be fired if a kiln is available. However, as with any clay, ALWAYS keep it wrapped in plastic so it doesn't dry out.

BUT ~ digging your own clay ~ stones and all ~ is more exciting! Investigate your locality for "pits". [The groundsman might find clay in your own school yard.] Is there a potter in the community who will accompany you on a "geology excursion" after rain? Scrape up handfuls of the clay into plastic bags. Clean up under the garden hose. Modelling is a natural activity, so students need little help. They soon learn not to make tails, noses, handles, and so on, too thin. Show them how to join pieces by "gluing" with wet clay [slip], pressing and smoothing parts together. Pot-making techniques such as pinching and coiling can be found in books.

Two pots made by pinching the clay into shape. YEAR 4

"Monument to Thought" YEAR 7

directed   **CLAY MODELLING**

Here is the opportunity to teach/consolidate —

 a) HOLLOW, SOLID, FLAT

and b) SAME ⟶ REPETITION
SIMILAR ⟶ HARMONY ⎱ See PRINCIPLES OF COMPOSITION
DIFFERENT ⟶ CONTRAST ⎰ TEACHER'S GUIDE, pp. 42-47.

1. Let's make certain types of shapes —

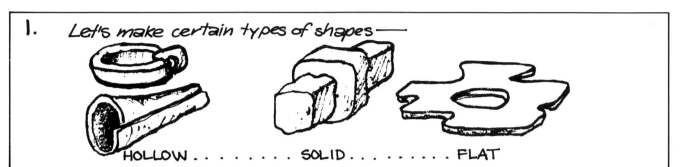

HOLLOW . . . . SOLID . . . . FLAT

2. Let's make some **FAMILIES** of shapes —

 ... all the **SAME**
 ↓
REPETITION of shape

 ... all **SIMILAR**
 ↓
HARMONY of shape

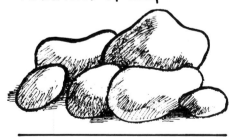

 ... all **DIFFERENT**
 ↓
CONTRAST of shape

CONSTRUCTION

FIRST, SOME TERMS TO LEARN FROM SCULPTURE ~

• <u>LOW RELIEF</u> : shapes protrude from flat background just enough to indicate the
shape ~ as in "Bubbles" below

• <u>HIGH RELIEF</u> : shapes protrude from background almost right around the shape
~ as in the heads of U.S Presidents at Mt. Rushmore.

• <u>FREE - STANDING or IN THE ROUND</u> : you can walk right around the shape and
view it from all positions ~ as in the Statue of Liberty.

---

24 low relief paper construction ~ cut some of the way around

shapes drawn on paper, and bend up to catch the light and shadows.

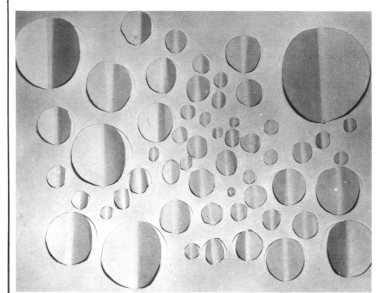

"FLIPS AND FLAPS"

Display on different coloured paper
and catch strong side light.

"BUBBLES" Year 10

25 free-standing construction

The partly finished piece of work at left, was started
by bending wire to form a figure, then stapling onto
a board. This supporting framework is called an
ARMATURE. Cotton wool was then glued around
it. This figure could be further developed by being
dipped into plaster of paris. [Buy at the hardware
store, but ask how to mix it.] If the figure is to be
painted, give it an undercoat of white Chromacryl
first.

CONSTRUCTION

YEAR 3

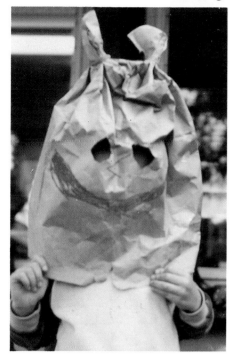

26 masks

need not be expensive or elaborate. Large bags will accommodate ears, whiskers, etc. with students using their own ingenuity. Provide them with scraps of wool, straws, rubber bands, dried grass, string, and so on. Chromacryl will come up in vibrant colours on brown paper. There are many exciting books available on masks.

YEAR 2

27 kites

Make some kites for the next windy day!

YEAR 1

28 paper maché

is time-consuming, but very rewarding ~ good for lunch-hour activities. The above shapes [strips of newsprint pasted over balloons] were used to learn the geography of the moon ~ its craters and seas.

29 mobiles

above were made by haphazardly cutting into large pieces of cartridge paper, painted with Chromacryl in the Primary colours. The unusual shapes were made by intertwining the pieces through themselves. They were hung with fishing line. On the right, is a more conventional type of mobile.

COLLAGE

YEAR 1   YEAR 5

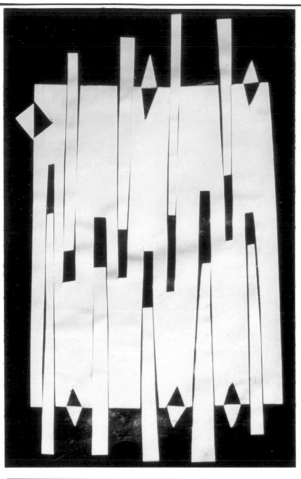

31 **mosaic** Glue any flat shapes, e.g. tiles, card, paper, shells, onto a background. Leave narrow spaces between the shapes.

30 **separation design** Start with a basic shape, e.g. a square, and cut in from the sides, taking a "bite" out of it ~ any shape. Keep in place on table. Glue the square onto a different coloured background, pulling the cut pieces out a little to leave spaces, and glue down, as in the sample above.

32 **fold-and-cut paper design**

Fold paper in two or four, cut or tear out pieces and glue, as on right. Hold folded paper in centre while cutting.

33 cloth collage

This work was based on the form of a TOTEM POLE. After studying Indian totem poles, the students decided that their design should also be **symmetrical** [the same on both sides of the centre line]. Young children may need to use shapes already cut.

Many children used symmetry of their own accord in later activities. Whether the word is remembered or not, is not as important as the understanding and application of the concept.

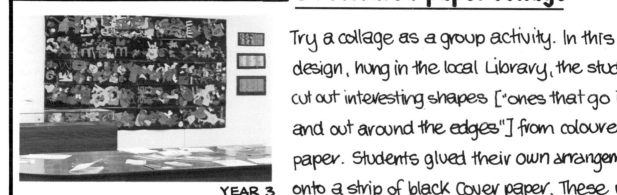
YEAR 3

34 coloured-paper collage

Try a collage as a group activity. In this design, hung in the local Library, the students cut out interesting shapes ["ones that go in and out around the edges"] from coloured paper. Students glued their own arrangements onto a strip of black cover paper. These were then joined together. The students learned the word **abstract**, as in "not meaning to look like any object". In the individual collage at left, abstract shapes were also used. One of the chief values of collage is that the student can explore arrangements and evaluate effects before gluing the shapes down. Each experience develops the aesthetic "taste" in design, and the awareness of the expressiveness of the abstract.

YEAR 2

COLLAGE

YEAR 6

35   The collage at left, is all about **SPATIAL RELATIONSHIPS** that give the effect of depth, ie. PERSPECTIVE. Cut out 6 trees or other objects [Contact is excellent], each smaller than the last, and stick them onto another coloured piece of paper, following these rules ~

(1.)   Place the SMALLEST near the top of the page ~ this will appear farthest away.

(2.)   Place all the others with the BASE of the shape going LOWER down the page the LARGER the shape to suggest their growing closer.

(3.)   Overlap some shapes, larger ones over the top of smaller, to suggest depth.

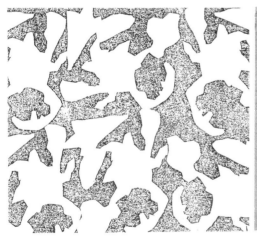

Try to see the dark areas as positive shapes with the white areas as space between.

YEAR 3

36 · 37   The above are about **POSITIVE** and **NEGATIVE SHAPES.** A negative shape is simply a space that can be looked at as a total shape with edges right around. At left, a pattern was made with the SAME shapes arranged to keep the spaces about the same area as the shapes, and as interesting. At right, SIMILAR and DIFFERENT shapes were used, based on a chair's theme. Both patterns are collages. For other approaches to producing negative shapes, see Activity 38, p.55 [opposite], Activity 39 b), p.56 and TONE, Activity 14, p.20.

pencil   DRAWING FROM LIFE

...TEACHES US TO **SEE** !!!

Simply set up the subject of
your choice and provide the
atmosphere for <u>CONCENTRATION</u>.

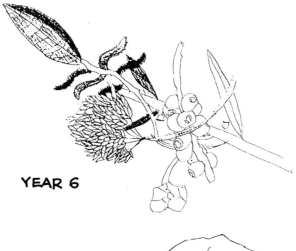

YEAR 6

YEAR 5

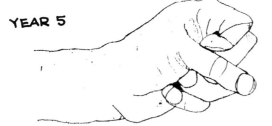

Students might like to select their own subjects.

YEAR 6

<u>PRACTISE SEEING NEGATIVE SHAPES IN LIFE</u> — carefully arrange several
objects, e.g. chairs, so the spaces between the parts form definite shapes. These
spaces are called negative shapes. It is easier if the students draw borders first,
for reference. Ask them to shade in each negative shape before proceeding to
the next. When finished, don't worry about "correct" representation of the
objects. If this exercise is too difficult, see Activity 39 b), next page.

DRAWING

some more ideas for drawing

Photograph: Shelley Munster, Queensland

- To help <u>IMAGINATION and VISUALIZATION</u>. Go back to Activity 13, a) and b) . Students close their eyes. Read out only half the paragraphs, then stop. Ask the students to draw what they are seeing in their imaginations, in their "minds' eyes". Try this with other stories or poems, and with music. This child is drawing to Bartok's Violin Concerto. The opening passages are very linear.

- To help see <u>NEGATIVE SHAPES</u>. Find a flat shape with holes in it. Draw the holes only, then add the shape around it.

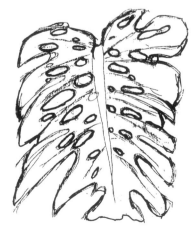

YEAR 5

- To help transfer <u>2D FORM</u> into <u>3D FORM</u>. Ask students to draw a shape on paper, then make it in clay.

PRINTING

40 thumb prints
Almost all flat objects are suitable for printing. The thumb prints in paint below have had lines added. These little fellows are crotchets and quavers, escapees from a song, enjoying their own fun.

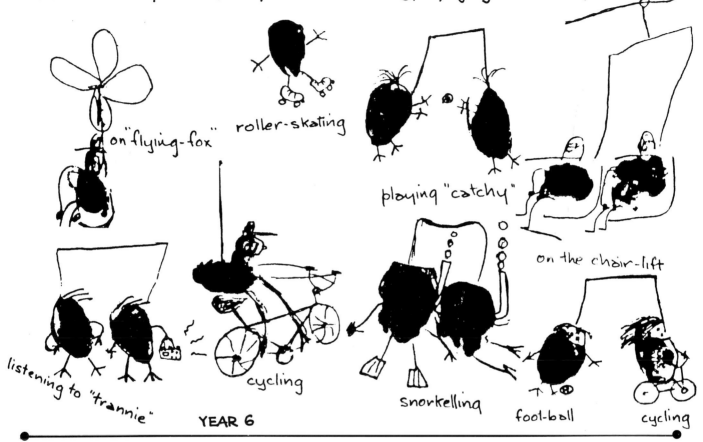

on "flying-fox"

roller-skating

playing "catchy"

on the chair-lift

listening to "trannie"

cycling

snorkelling

foot-ball

cycling

YEAR 6

41 stencil
produces positive shapes.

YEAR 6

Cut shape <u>out</u> of paper [folded] and paint over with brush or roller.

42 template
produces negative shapes.

YEAR 6

Place cut shape on paper and paint over with brush or roller. Remove shape.

SHAPE 57

PAINTING

This is the area in which students tend to be most stifled by their non-artist teachers, as they were stifled by their teachers before them. If you are a non-artist teacher, the following may provide a few important guidelines.

• Take care <u>not</u> to nurture the "draw and colour-in" approach as the <u>only</u> way to paint. Do many paintings without prior drawing. It usually isn't until about Year 3 that children feel the need to "draw up first". This is when the peer pressure attacks their confidence. Develop ways of expressing the act of painting such as, "talk with paint", "move with the ideas in your paintings", "instead of words, tell us in paint", " let the feelings or the character of the subject, flow through your brush."

• <u>Praise all genuine attempts</u>! Encourage the attitude that a painting is <u>not</u> "wrecked" at any stage ~ it simply ISN'T FINISHED! Try washing it under the tap, then touching it up. Because Chromacryl is opaque, you can paint layer over layer. Draw over it with pastel, crayon or ink. Turn it into something else ~ a collage or paper plane. <u>Then</u>, try again. Remember, few professionals complete a work at a single sitting. Some take years!

• Join in the painting yourself. Enjoy it with the students. Share with them in something that isn't just "right" or "wrong".

PAINTING

some suggestions for shapely subjects

a) Set up a **STILL-LIFE** group of interesting objects. Draw it in ink with a twig for a pen, in pencil, or in charcoal. Add a few touches of colour with paint or other colour medium. Colours do not have to match objects, of course.

b) **ILLUSTRATE A STORY** ~ the child's own, or a group or class story. Make a book using the photocopier to duplicate copies for the Library, for the class, and one for some little old lady. [Paintings usually reproduce well.]

c) Go **OUTDOORS** and paint from life, but not on a windy day! Add other shapes...Ned Kelly? Santa Claus? monsters? space module? more trees?

d) Remember a **FEELING** you had very strongly ~ fear, anger, excitement, boredom ~ and paint it. You don't have to put yourself in it. You may like to use just colours and abstract shapes.

e) Remember some **EVENT** when some **OBJECT** was important. Tell us about it in paint. Make sure the object stands out well.

f) Just **DOODLE** some shapes in paint – any technique. Add any other medium [tissue paper? cellophane? sand?] and see what happens. You might get an idea along the way, or maybe not. Enjoy the experience of experimenting.

PAINTING

YEAR 1

◀ Children usually start painting by using shapes like words, written anywhere on the paper. Encourage the painting of the whole surface so that the whole page comes alive ~ but only if the child <u>wants</u> it to.

◀ <u>If</u> a student becomes disgruntled because the drawing has been lost and everything is "a mess", LET IT DRY, then.

YEAR 5

◀ ... go over the paint with more Chromacryl, ink [with a twig for a pen], pastels, crayon, or other medium [see top right photograph, COLOUR, p.45], or cut out shapes from Contact or ordinary paper and glue down over the painted background. Often these "saved" pictures turn out more interesting than the first intended one. Let the students learn this.

"Rain on my Roof"

YEAR 2

FROTTAGE

YEAR 3

Cut cardboard shapes and place under newsprint or other thin paper. Hold flat charcoal on its side and stroke gently over places where the shapes are. Move shapes around if desired to make a herd of elephants, a parade of people, a field of flowers . . . See the TEACHER'S GUIDE, p. 44, LINE, p. 55. TONE, p. 43 [YEAR 5] and TEXTURE, p. 37.

AND...

"DOING YOUR OWN thing" TIME

Give..., as many opportunities as possible for students to select their **own subjects**, their **own media and techniques** and their **own time limits** ~ perhaps in short sessions over several days. Or, have a whole session for the class, **teacher** included. Invite any interested **parents**. They often appreciate their children's work so much more when they have participated themselves.

SECTION THREE

Evaluation

OBSERVE the student at work ~ to assess confidence, self-reliance, application of knowledge, manipulative skills, work habits, and so on.

"ARE YOU HAPPY WITH WHAT YOU HAVE DONE, ALLISON?"

DOES THE STUDENT NEED HELP?

TALK to the student ~ establish the intentions and compare with results. Was the selection of medium, techniques and types of shapes suitable for the subject? Were the intentions directed toward the REALISTIC RECORD, the EXPERIMENTAL, INTELLECTUAL, IMAGINATIVE, DECORATIVE, AESTHETIC, or as a PERSONAL EXPRESSION ~ or as PRACTICE? See pp. 64-71.

"WHAT IS IT ABOUT, KYLIE?" "WHY DID YOU USE THOSE SHAPES, WENDY?"

LOOK at the student's work in relation to all experiences covered so far. Has knowledge been applied? TAKE THE WORK HOME. GIVE IT A GOOD "SEEING" ~ READ IT AS IF IT WAS WRITTEN TO YOU PERSONALLY. Every mark a student makes means something, so don't miss it.

COMPARE the student's work with previous work. Is he or she trying _new_ things or simply repeating "successful" formulae?

See <u>EVALUATION</u> section in the <u>TEACHER'S GUIDE</u>, pp. 57-59.

What to look for —

See TEACHER'S GUIDE
PP. 50-55.

DON'T FORGET TO CONSIDER THE TEMPERAMENTS. There's the slap-dash and the laborious, the meek and the bumptious. One is no better or worse than the other ~ just different. Try to appreciate the differences.

REALISTIC RECORD
Sue YEAR 1

◀ Note the addition of strokes and dashes to fill the empty spaces ~ a common "device". Show students how to paint backgrounds in fully so they have a choice.

Jason YEAR 4

The painting from life above, has all the life and enthusiasm of the <u>direct style</u> of young children. The drawing from imagination on the right, indicates the "studio-based" <u>application of knowledge</u> of perspective and light and shade. Ensure the students acquire BOTH, so they can choose which approach they want. Realistic records need not be photographic to be "true" to the artist.

The collage of a tree below was made from arranging shapes cut from a large sheet on which the child experimented with printing techniques using paint and rollers, before attempting Activities 41,42, p.57. By making use of experimental work, the student learns to "keep an eye open" for the potential use of future practice or experimental work. Professional artists, by taking experimental work seriously in this way, often discover techniques and media which can become their hallmarks. Students and teachers often tend to think experimental work is just for throwing away when completed. When possible, cut out some particularly effective section and display it. See COLOUR, p.49. Also see the TEACHER'S GUIDE, p.18 ~ "exploring visually", "a jig-saw puzzle tree."

Narelle YEAR 5

INTELLECTUAL RECORD

These samples of <u>ONE POINT</u> and <u>TWO POINT PERSPECTIVE</u> show how children can manage perspective, providing they are not confused with abstruse explanations of the phenomenon. It is a case of their following simple directions and seeing that **it works**. [Try it for Year 5 and upwards.]

ONE POINT PERSPECTIVE

1. Draw the horizon line [where land meets sky].
2. Put a point on the horizon near the centre.
3. Draw the **whole front side** of box that faces you. [See dark lines.]
4. Draw all lines GOING AWAY FROM YOU, to the centre point.

5. Draw in horizontal back edge and vertical sides. Rub out unwanted lines.

TWO POINT PERSPECTIVE

1. Draw horizon.
2. Put 2 points on the horizon, one on left, one on right.
3. Draw **front vertical edge**. [See dark lines.]
4. Draw all lines GOING AWAY FROM YOU, to left and right points.
5. Draw in all the vertical edges. Make sure these <u>are</u> vertical — it is easy to make them lean over.

N.B. Make this a fun exercise. Students should not feel obliged to use it in their future work.

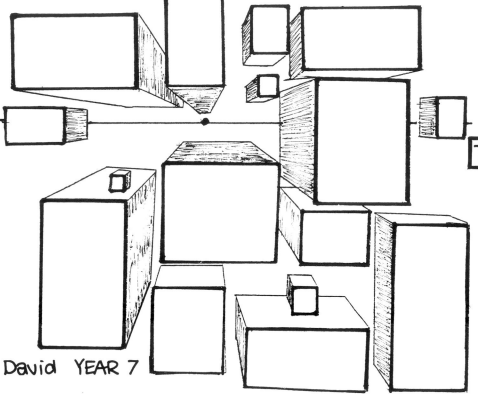

David YEAR 7

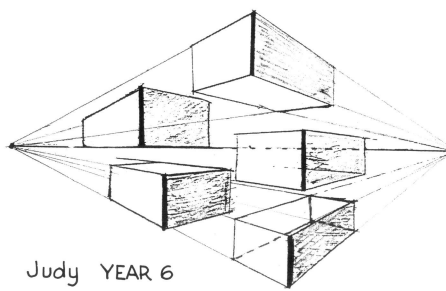

Judy YEAR 6

"THE MXAPOBOT"

An event in the life of A SHAPE ~

the Mxapobot

Melinda YEAR 5

A great deal of sensitivity to feelings is expressed in this cartoon ~ uncertainity, fright, fear, sorrow and compassion ~ all in pithy and logical sequence. [can you spot the inconsistency?] The use of the cartoon "movement lines" was part of the exercise, after observing these in professional work. Children appreciate such artwork in their own world after trying it themselves. [A delightful touch was added at the end ~ the Mxapobot was given pink blushing cheeks for embarrassment!]

In the drawing at right, observe how the child had less trouble drawing his imaginative trip to the Ecrtomnac [his own term], than in writing it. What marvellous confidence in the line work, with no need for an eraser to rub out "mistakes". The child knows there's no need to rub out overlapping cloud lines ~ he's telling a story "for heaven's sakes!"

Ben YEAR I

Went To the oTEcrtomnac
and we oTEcrtomnac Look AT the
oTEcrtomnac

Julie YEAR 7

For the design above, the children explored decorative pattern, using REPETITION
of shape but with variation in some way [in this case, size]. Also, the children explored a technique involving the application of Craypas [or other soft crayon]
along the edges of paper shapes, putting these one by one onto the page and
smearing the colours outward from the shape with the thumb or finger. To
evaluate this work on a decorative level, notice how the child put down the
pattern of large fish first, then overlapped with small fish, filling up empty
spaces. Some of the smaller fish overlap each other as well, giving an effect
of low relief depth. [see p.50] Further variety is produced by the change
of direction of the fish, large and small. Also, there is a good feeling of
UNITY with the more interesting pattern of small fish concentrated near the
centre. [For definitions of REPETITION and UNITY, see the TEACHER'S
GUIDE, pp. 42, 43 and pp. 36, 37 respectively.]

Ben YEAR 6

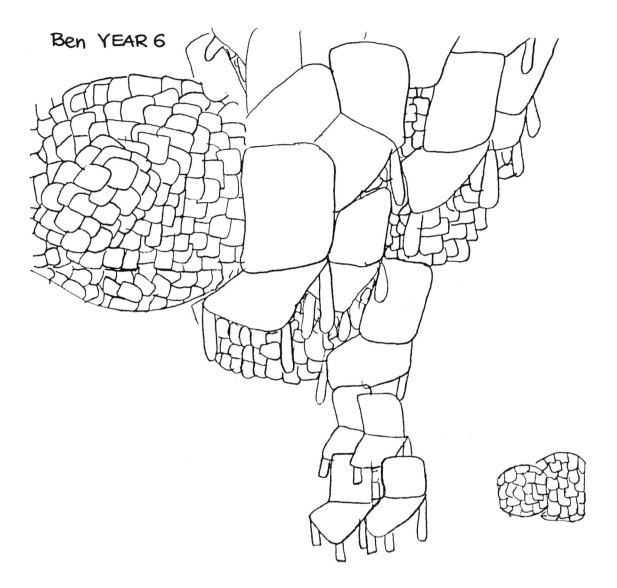

This work is a development of Activity 8, p.22, when the children drew shapes from life, outdoors and indoors. This collection was to provide a starting point for compositions that were felt to be aesthetically pleasing. The children selected any number of shapes from the collection and arranged them together so they **LOOKED GOOD**, i.e. aesthetically pleasing. See the TEACHER'S GUIDE, p.21, and also the sculpture design on p.38 of the same booklet. The most ingenious aspect of the design above is that innumerable shapes have been held together by overlapping and setting in a "gel" of squares [the television screen] to make one shape ~ with a feeling of downward movement and filtering out. The floating shape added on the lower right serves to balance out the left-hand heaviness of the main shape. As with almost every other sample of work in this program, this is the child's first attempt at the activity. What will the future hold?

Peter YEAR 5

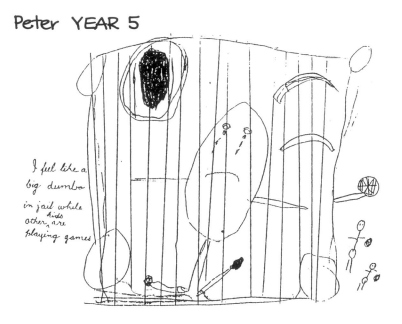

I feel like a big dumbo in jail while other kids are playing games

In both samples on this page, the children were asked to remember some occasion when they felt very strongly about something, e.g. when they were frightened or excited [Activity 43 d), p.59]. When evaluating such work, we need to accept interpretations of a situation in the same way as a listener.

Above, the child has used symbols for his feelings of inadequacy during games times. His own potato-like shape is "dumbo" in essence, the jail seems symbolic of his being trapped and somehow punished for his lack of adequacy. The figures outside are small and far away.

Leo YEAR 3

Above is a "Running on Rainbows" version of the stale, traditional, "Day at the Beach" subject ~ let loose, with a goodly measure of JOY!

Michael YEAR 7

The above drawings of the teacher have been done without looking down at the paper. In the first, the pencil is not lifted throughout. In the second, the pencil is lifted to start a new line whenever it is felt necessary. Correct proportions are _not_ important, although, with practice, the eye and hand will co-ordinate together and almost perfect proportions can be achieved. When evaluating these pieces, look to see how many details the child has seen and depicted. It is obvious when he or she has just drawn what is known rather than seen. It is a valuable concentration exercise in seeing and co-ordination rather than a means to an end product.

See LINE, Activity 19, p. 50.

Australian potter, Kevin Grealy, demonstrating at the Mytton House Galleries' Summer School, Warwick, Queensland. See Student's Book, p.16.

Colour

COLOUR TERMS for the teacher

For Colour Study with the students, see pp. 36-38

PRIMARY COLOURS... YELLOW, RED, BLUE. These colours cannot be made by mixing any other colours.

SECONDARY COLOURS... ORANGE, PURPLE, VIOLET, GREEN. These colours are made by mixing pairs of Primary colours:

yellow + red = orange

red + blue = purple [more reddish]

blue + red = violet [more bluish]

blue + yellow = green

TERTIARY COLOURS... made by mixing pairs of Secondary colours. They are always "muddy" colours, e.g. brown.

[An easy way to mix brown?........ add a little black to orange or mix all three Primaries together.]

TONE [or VALUE]... the degree of LIGHTNESS or DARKNESS of a colour. Light colours: HIGH tone. Dark: LOW tone

INTENSITY... the degree of BRIGHTNESS or DULLNESS of a colour. Bright colours: HIGH intensity. Dull: LOW intensity

---

HUE... a colour at its brightest, e.g. all the colours on the colour wheel.

TINT... a hue mixed with **WHITE**, e.g. pink is a tint of red, mauve is a tint of violet.

SHADE... a hue mixed with **BLACK**, e.g. maroon is a shade of red, navy is a shade of blue.

GREYED [or NEUTRALIZED] **COLOUR**... a hue mixed with GREY [black + white] or the colour opposite on the colour wheel e.g. green + purple.

N.B. The definitions of Harmony and Discord below, are not accepted by all schools of Art.

THE " NATURAL ORDER " OF COLOURS ... is the order of the tones of

colours. Following the colours as on the colour wheel [see p. 36] ~ yellow is
the lightest, violet is the darkest, and the colours either side of yellow grow
step by step darker towards violet. So yellow is "naturally" lighter than blue.

HARMONY OF COLOUR ... this is produced when colours in their "natural

order" are side by side, e.g. when red and violet are used, the violet is
darker, [even when versions of these are used, e.g. pale pink and darker
mauve. Remember, pink is a tint of red, mauve is a tint of violet.]

DISCORD OF COLOUR ... this is produced when colours that are NOT in

their "natural order" are side by side, e.g. when red and violet are
used, and the red is darker, ie. when the red is used as a shade
[maroon] and the violet is used as a tint [mauve]. Discord, such as
maroon and mauve, is not "wrong". It is only "discordant" in this
theory. Nature uses it, e.g. pale blue flowers on dark green shrubs.
With colours the same tone, e.g. red and green, make one very dark
and one very light to produce discord. Do remember that, in this theory,
the word "discord" has no association with unpleasantness.

Harmony is often defined as occurring when colours used all contain a common colour.

TYPES OF COLOUR SCHEMES

MONOCHROMATIC ... the use of a number of colours based on the ONE
hue, e.g. red, pinks, maroons. [ie. tints, shades, and
neutralized versions of the one hue]. See p. 38.

NEIGHBOURING [or ADJACENT, or ANALOGOUS] ... the use of
colours that are NEXT TO EACH OTHER on the colour
wheel, e.g. yellow, orange and red [or tints and shades of these].

CONTRASTING ... the use of colours that are OPPOSITE each other, or
nearly so, e.g. orange and blue. [For COMPLEMENTARY, or
the exact opposite, stare at a patch of bright colour, then
stare at a white sheet of paper - you will see the complementary!]

Colour

Colour comes from outside me ~ with the light. When it comes with morning, it lifts me and I rise above all things. It wraps me around warmly with its yellows, or sets me free. And through the day, colours come and go, pass by, or close me in; they natter gently or drone with dullness, or glare or giggle with brightness; and then with night, press down in deep coolness, and release me into darkness.

Contents

SUGGESTED WORK PLAN FOR A BLOCK UNIT OF 10 WEEKS ON COLOUR

Mix 'n' match your own activities if not using the plan below. Be flexible!
Omit or extend activities where desired or practical. See N.B. LINE, p.5.

WEEK ONE

AWARENESS: Talking colour – ACTIVITY 1...pp.10·11. Vocabulary brainstorming

Seeing colour – ACTIVITY 2...p.12. Seeing Safari

PRACTICAL: Experimental "play"– ACTIVITY 16...p.32. Painting

WEEK TWO

AWARENESS: Seeing colour – ACTIVITY 3...pp.13·14. Audio-visuals · Display

Integration – ACTIVITY 10 a)...p.22. Projector activity

PRACTICAL: Directed experience– ACTIVITY 17...pp.33·34. Painting techniques

Applied experience– ACTIVITY 18...p.35. Painting

WEEK THREE

AWARENESS: Seeing colour – ACTIVITY 4...p.15. Appreciation · Student's Book

ACTIVITY 11 b)...p.23. Cellophane collage · Video

PRACTICAL: Other media – ACTIVITY 23·24...pp.40·41. Cellophane collage

WEEK FOUR

AWARENESS: Seeing colour – ACTIVITY 5...p.17. Select an activity/ies

ACTIVITY 7...p.19. Colour display

Integration – ACTIVITY 14...pp.26·27. Writing. Select activity

PRACTICAL: Colour study – ACTIVITY 20·22...pp.37·39. Roller prints · Dyeing

WEEK FIVE

AWARENESS: Integration – ACTIVITY 10 b) · 11 c) and 11 d)...pp.22·23

Combine above in one session

PRACTICAL: Colour study – ACTIVITY 19...p.36. Colour wheel · Rainbows

WEEK SIX

AWARENESS: Seeing colour – ACTIVITY 4...p.16. Appreciation · Student's Book

PRACTICAL: Colour study – { ACTIVITY 21...p.38. Monochromatic painting

Seeing colour – { ACTIVITY 8...p.20. Painting · Combine with above

N.B. The time spent on any of the AWARENESS EXPERIENCES can vary from 5 mins. to
40 mins., to a life-time's interest ~ according to age, stage, and time available.

WEEK SEVEN			
AWARENESS:	Integration	—	ACTIVITY 12...p.24. Choreograph in colour
			ACTIVITY 13...p.25. Listening to colour
PRACTICAL:	Other media	—	ACTIVITY 27...p.43. Group painting

WEEK EIGHT			
AWARENESS:	Integration	—	ACTIVITY 9...p.21. Colour in drama
	Other media	—	ACTIVITY 25...p.41. Paper collage

WEEK NINE			
AWARENESS:	Seeing colour	—	ACTIVITY 14...p.28. Writing. Scripts. Ethnic
	Integration	—	ACTIVITY 6...p.18. Select an activity/ies
PRACTICAL:	Other media	—	ACTIVITY 28...p.44. Puppets

WEEK TEN			
AWARENESS:	Integration	—	ACTIVITY 15...pp.29·30. Word Display
	Language of colour	—	ACTIVITY 11f)...p.23. Video Show
PRACTICAL:	Other media	—	ACTIVITY 26...p.42. Painted objects
			ACTIVITY 29...pp.45·46. "Doing your own thing" time

N.B. Remember that the above Work Plan is a suggested one only. The whole Program is designed to be flexible, so some activities can be omitted, adapted or extended. The same Activity may take 10 minutes or an hour. The most important aspect is that **AWARENESS EXPERIENCES** are to work hand in hand with **PRACTICAL EXPERIENCES** so that students have a source for their ideas. Also, the build-up of **VOCABULARY** is important for aesthetic development, and **DRAWING FROM LIFE** essential for learning to "see".

Daily Drawing Books often provide teachers with much needed moments

of peace! Even the most unruly students consider them their own private "Art studios", and will concentrate avidly while drawing. Let them draw whatever they wish. [Drawings of dubious moral tone, of course, have no place in it. Take a "no fuss, but no go" stance.] Students are usually proud of their work, so do take an interest in it. Photocopy interesting work. See LINE, p.69 and TONE pp.42, 44. **DO TRY IT!**

Materials

THE BASIC KIT
— double if possible

CHROMACRYL PAINT — all five colours* ... PP. 28 · 32 - 39 · 42 · 43 · 46

CELLOPHANE - 16 pkts - RED^8 [dark], BLUE^4, and YELLOW^4,
pp. 23 · 26 · 40 · 41

COLOURED PAPER — $\frac{1}{2}$ pkt matt squares - 254^2 mm ... p. 41

GLUE [powdered] → $\frac{1}{2}$ litre ... p. 41

Also, if possible —   CLEAR PLASTIC SHEETING, 2-6m .... p. 40 (37)

BLACK PLASTIC SHEETING, 2-6 m ... p. 41 (37)

CRAYPAS - 10 boxes ... pp. 22 · 33 · 34

THE BARE BONES KIT

CHROMACRYL PAINT - all five colours* ... pp. 28 · 32 - 39 · 42 · 43 · 46

CELLOPHANE - 8 pkts - RED^4 [dark], BLUE^2, and YELLOW^2,
pp. 23 · 26 · 40 · 41

Also, if possible — COLOURED PAPER — 1 pkt matt squares - 254^2 mm.
... p. 41

CRAYPAS - 5 pkts .... pp. 22 · 33 · 34

SCAVENGE/SAVE UP FOR — CLEAR PLASTIC SHEETING - 2-6m ... p. 40

BLACK PLASTIC SHEETING - 2-6m ... p. 41

MAKE YOUR OWN — FLOUR and WATER GLUE ... p. 41

THE *running on* . . . THIN AIR KIT

CHROMACRYL PAINT — all five colours* .. pp. 28 · 32 - 39 · 42 · 43 · 46

SCAVENGE, SAVE AND MAKE YOUR OWN, AS FOR ABOVE KITS

FOR ALL KITS :   ● Collection of scraps of coloured cloth — or discarded articles of clothing,
scarves particularly — keep patterned pieces separate ... pp. 10 · 11 · 19 · 24

● Collection of old coloured clothes for drama ... p. 21

* Commercial names : Cool Yellow, Warm Red, Warm Blue, Black, White.

SECTION ONE

Awareness experiences

AIMS:
- to awaken an interest in colour **for its own sake**
- to develop a **vocabulary** about colour at all levels of awareness ~ physical to abstract

- TALKING COLOUR
- SEEING COLOUR
- INTEGRATED EXPERIENCES WITH COLOUR
- LANGUAGE OF COLOUR

RESOURCES

RESOURCES: Make a permanent collection of scraps of plain coloured cloth with a great variety of colours. Coloured paper is also suitable but does not withstand constant handling.

For colour displays such as the "washing line" below, whole pieces of clothing can be used. You may need to add a little colour to your wardrobe!

See p. 19.

VOCABULARY BRAINSTORMING

BRAINSTORM!

Students can sit in a circle.

Distribute the pieces of coloured cloth.

QUESTION, COMMENT, **COLLECT WORDS**.

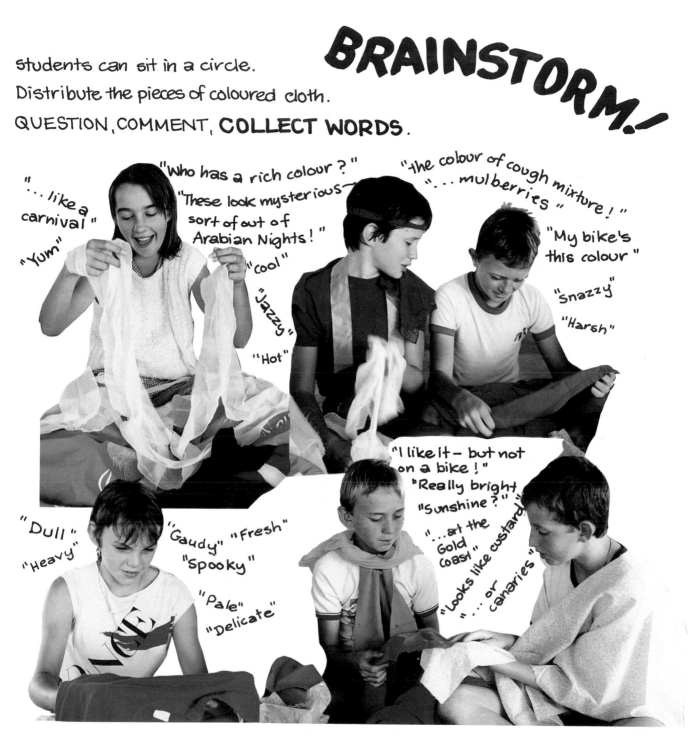

"... like a carnival"

"Yum"

"Who has a rich colour ?"

"These look mysterious — sort of out of Arabian Nights !"

"cool"

"Jazzy"

"Hot"

"the colour of cough mixture !"

"... mulberries"

"My bike's this colour"

"snazzy"

"Harsh"

"Dull"

"Heavy"

"Gaudy" "Fresh"

"spooky"

"Pale"

"Delicate"

"I like it – but not on a bike !"

"Really bright"

"Sunshine ?"

"... at the Gold Coast"

"Looks like custard"

"... or canaries"

A teacher-aide or parent might help to put these words onto **WORD CARDS** for displays. Keep them for future years' resources. Keep a list also. Metaphors and similes should be easy to elicit ~ "As red as a ... lobster ? beetroot ? rose ?" Develop these clichés into <u>new</u> ideas ~ "As red as ... a raw steak? Red Riding Hood's cape ? rooster's comb? embarrassment red ?" **CHECK WITH P.30 SO YOU ARE WELL ARMED WITH WORDS YOURSELF.**

THE SEEING SAFARI

AIMS:
- to help the students learn to ˋSEE´, i.e. to see **more** than the mere physical presence of objects
- to develop further a **VOCABULARY** about colour on all levels of awareness ~ physical to abstract

Go on a safari in the schoolyard or down the road. Take your camera - with colour film in it — to collect resources. Simply point out and discuss the colours around you. How many different greens can you see? Is the sky the same blue all over? Are tree trunks really all brown? Are all leaves green? Where is the brightest colour? Who can see some puce? [Oxford dictionary: flea-colour, purple-brown.] On the same day or another occasion give students a piece of coloured cloth or paper and send them on a colour hunt to find something that matches, or nearly matches. One or two students could do this.

START COLLECTING THE WORDS USED! see pp. 29, 30.

lemon green · strong green · intense green · rich green · faded green · bold green · luminous green · pale green · fresh green · delicate green · emerald green · insipid green · muted green · bluish green · lime green · shady green · cool green · jungle green · greyish green · mustard green · yellowish green · lively green · sea green · dark green · light green · dead green · sickly green

. . . just greens!

INTRODUCE SOME NEW WORDS —
eg. bold, murky, delicate, subtle, muted

MAKING THE MOST OF MEDIA

AUDIO-VISUAL RESOURCES:

For colour study, use cellophane on the overhead projector. Ensure you have intense hues of the Primary colours, e.g. rich red rather than a tint of pink. Several layers may be needed to make the hue. Use only the Primary colours but overlay them to make other colours.

Investigate sources of videos, films, strips, etc. about COLOUR, and/or make some yourself. Ask school and community Libraries, Education Centres, Film Centres, and so on.

Check the school television and radio broadcasts for Art programs. Timetables are usually available at the beginning of each year. Try to build up the school's resources as well as your own.

WATCH AND DISCUSS.

STATIC RESOURCES:

See next page.

LOOK AND DISCUSS.

DISPLAY in the classroom, or elsewhere in the school ~

- photographs you, or others, have taken
- pictures from magazines
- newspaper photographs
- posters
- record covers, book covers, and so on.

You may have space for only **ONE** photograph in your classroom ~ fine! It will have unrivalled status of importance ~ but do change it often.

MEDIA   classroom display

COLOUR AROUND THE WORLD

Make a display of photographs from someone's overseas trip.

◄ Bright, contrasting colours of a street market in Dublin, Ireland.

◄ Mellow, soft and subtle colours of roofs in Assissi, in central Italy.

◄ Colours of fun and festivity at Expo '86 in Vancouver, Canada.

APPRECIATION IN THE WORLD OF ART

DISCUSS the Art works below in conjunction with the Student's Book, pp. 7, 14 and 15.

127 x 101.6 cm

Courtesy of the Tasmanian Museum and Art Gallery

"SNAKE BAY AT NIGHT" by Russell DRYSDALE. [1912-1981 AUST.] Oil on canvas. 1959

Stained-glass window in the Votive Cathedral, Vienna, Austria.

When discussing interesting points [just one or two will do] of Art with students, it often helps to put two works side by side and **compare**. Black outlines around colour patches are obvious in both works above. The way stained-glass is made, with lead strips to hold the glass, necessitates the outline. But has Drysdale used black outlines to make his painting like a cathedral, a place of worship? Note the "coming and going", the "lost and found" of figures, grave posts and distant landscape.

This delightful hippopotamus comes from Ancient Egypt. He is adorned with lotus flowers and birds of the Nile River. Work such as this is an instant "success" and helps to prove to students that Art from the adult world is not "stuffy" or beyond their appreciation. Try to collect reproductions of such gems.

Courtesy of Kunsthistoriches Museum, Vienna

APPRECIATION IN THE WORLD AROUND US

The importance of Tone in colour

See Student's Book, p. 6.

Below are sections of a marvellous side-walk mural in Cordelia St., South Brisbane, Queensland, painted by over 200 people of different ethnic groups, as part of Fiesta '87, a project by the Migrant Resource Centre, Brisbane.

Administrators: Penny Glass and Sergio Aldunate. Co-ordinators: Vanessa Fisher, Maria Filipow and Mark Crocker.

This mural is in colour, so there are no problems of clarity ... except IF
i) viewed from a very long distance away, or
ii) photographed in black and white.

Note how the emu, at left, 'disappears' because its dark colours are almost the same as the dark background. Most of the lower photo-graph shows strong defini-tion because of the strong CONTRAST of tones.

[You can convert colour into black and white also by turning the colour on and off on the television set.]

Tonal contrasts are important for newspaper photographers, who work in black and white. It is possible for a black and white photograph to be almost blank if the colours in real life are exactly the same tone. Try a painting in which all the colours [different colours, e.g. red, green] are the SAME TONE. Add black or white to make colours darker or lighter. Photocopy it in black and white. Is it blank?

APPRECIATION IN THE STUDENT'S OWN WORLD

Fun 'n' Games with colour

IDEAS FOR MORE COLOUR AWARENESS

- Find some games involving colour. The students may know some already. The Librarian may know of some table games. Encourage the playing of these games at lunch-times.

- Designate colours to groups in the class ~ the Gingers, the Jades and the Jets, and so on. Organize timetables through colour ~ Green for Wednesday, sport Practice, etc. Turn the reading corner of the room into a warm-colours area ~ yellows, oranges, reds, purples. Find ways to involve colour in the room organization.

- Have a day when the students can wear clothes of their favourite colour, or of any bright colours. Or, if this is not feasible, they might like to bring along an object that features their favourite colour or colour scheme.

- Try quick memory games. "What colour eyes does Tracey have?" "What colour is your front door?"

- If students watch television at home, ask them to select the commercial that appeals to them most in colour. Perhaps it will be just a single shot. Discuss these at school next day, so that the students can observe these commercials again at home, aware of other students' preferences. Explain carefully it is not the content they are looking for, but the colour.

- Try a game of who can think of the most names of famous people, groups, songs, towns, countries, stories, etc. involving the name of a colour, e.g. Erik the Red [Viking], Greenland, Little Red Riding Hood ...

APPRECIATION OF THE OUTSIDE WORLD

colours of Other Cultures

- Study the use of ochres by Australian Aborigines. Make some ochres. Simply mix water with different coloured clays.
- Make use of special dates. St Patrick's Day can turn a whole school green, leaving an indelible memory in the child's mind!
- Find parents to discuss colours of their own ethnic group. And "down-town"... any red and green Chinese restaurants?
- Need we mention the inspirational effect of colours in sporting "cultures"? Discuss also, school colours, flags, club colours, and so on.

Colourful folk art, Indian beads from Colorado, U.S.A.

Aboriginal ochre pits near Alice Springs, N.T., AUST.

A London "bobby" decorated in colours identifying the street marchers as a group.

Fijian firewalkers in traditional, colourful dress.

COLOURS ON CENTRE STAGE

● MAKE A COLOUR COLLAGE

Glue a collection of scraps of coloured materials onto a backing. Scraps can be collected from home or from clothing factories. Give the colour display a title such as A CARNIVAL OF COLOURS, or a subject such as the illustration at right.

OR ... Instead of using glue, bring out the sewing machine! If students are too young to use the machine, find a willing parent. Or, students can sew pieces of cloth on by hand. Sewing need not be "expert"!

e.g. JOSEPH'S COAT OF MANY COLOURS

● OR

HANG OUT YOUR WASHING!

Overlap colours so there are no gaps.

HARSH · YUM · COOL · DULL · YUK · WARM · RED AS A TOMATO · BRIGHT · MAUVE

see p. 10

Pin words or phrases onto the cloth. Add to them now and again. Remember to cover expressive phrases, e.g. "riotous red", "sombre grey", "blue as the miseries", and a few "big" words, e.g. "insipid", "flamboyant", "luminous". Students can make a collection display, also, on a table, with objects.

RECORDING COLOURS FROM LIFE

PAINTING FROM LIFE ...TEACHES US TO SEE!!✓

* It is recommended that Activities 16 and 17 be done before this activity.

a) a still life

Very simply set up a colourful subject of flowers, pieces of cloth, teapot, objects that belong to the students, etc. Do not worry if the students cannot match the colours, or even that they don't try to. If they <u>want</u> to but cannot, you need to teach them colour mixing. See Activity 20, 21 and 22, pp. 37-39 and p.48. See also SHAPE, pp. 59 and 64, and the TEACHER'S GUIDE, pp. 26, 27.

b) outdoor painting — FIND AN INTERESTING PLACE

This activity takes more organization than the above, but the students enjoy it immensely and it covers so much more than the still-life activity. Creating the effect of distance is quite an accomplishment and there are "rules" and "hints" that can be followed. However, at this stage, it is quite adequate just to enjoy the experience. If possible, find an assistant ~ or two ~ so that materials are already in place when the students arrive and the final tidying up can be checked over satisfactorily. Older students should be able to attend to their own organization. Only one warning ~ don't try it in windy weather! Even Chromacryl can't stop paper blowing away!

USING COLOUR IN DRAMA

✳ let's dress up

Collect clothes, pieces of material, etc. with a good variety of colour. Students can make up impromptu plays, dressing up to suit their character. It may be easier to dress up first, then see what sort of characters have been created. Give some starter ideas, e.g. Vince the Villain tells little Priscilla Prettycurl that her neighbour, old Mrs Doreen Drearybones, is really an outcast from another planet. How does Priscilla find out if this is true?

black beret
black moustache
bright red scarf
black coat

pink bow

frilly dress in pale pastel colours

Sound effects can be added to suit the characters

Here are some common associations—

white ..... pure, perfect, clean

black ...... villainous, threatening

red .... fiery, exciting

yellow ..... cheerful, sunny

green ...... cool, relaxing

purple ..... royal, mysterious

blue ...... free, light-hearted

orange ... warm, friendly

brown .... grubby, earthy

grey ...... dull, boring

On right, is a scene from the Barong Dance, Bali. The black and white checks symbolize the presence of both good and evil.

Photograph: John Thorpe, Tasmania

WATCHING COLOUR

✳ colour on the move

SOME IDEAS . . . WHICH MAY LEAD TO OTHER IDEAS

a) Set up the slide projector in a darkened room. Find some colourful slides ~ of anything. Project these UPSIDE DOWN, on moving students. The students could suggest movements suitable for the colours, e.g. greens . . . swaying forest trees. This activity could follow Activity 3, p.13, after watching slides. It can be very effective!

b) Fill clear glass bottles or clear plastic cups with water. Drop food colouring or powdered food dye, cloth dye, or paint [red, yellow and blue] into each. Mix colours and watch them change. This is fascinating in the sun. Place containers on white paper and observe transmitted colour on the paper.

c) Using a small electric fan, tape a square of paper, patterned with bright colours [paint, Craypas], to the centre and rotate. Will the pattern change? Will the colours change?

WATCHING COLOUR

✻ capture it on video

SOME IDEAS FOR SIMPLE, MAGIC EFFECTS

a) Film a student painting ~ any design or painting with many colours. Chromacryl dries quickly, will take many layers, and has vibrant colours, so is very effective for the job.
Then... **show it backwards!!** Watch the colours disappear!

b) Sticky-tape pieces of different coloured cellophane over a window pane where the light is strong. Film students moving on the other side through the cellophane. Move the camera around also, to pick up the different colours. Try zooming in. Add a voice over, "This is John, yellow all over, in Springtime...". See p.4.

c) Film the spectrum made by a glass prism from the science equipment, at close range. Try some symmetrical patterns using a mirror against the prism. This is visually very exciting. If no video camera is available, just observe.

d) Film the colours in the clear containers shown on the page opposite, as the colours are being added.

e) Film the bright colours around the school, then the dull colours.

f) Have a **COLOUR SHOW** with all you have filmed above. Make invitations and invite other classes, teachers, parents, the Principal ~ and don't forget the cleaner, if available!

MOVING WITH COLOUR IN MUSIC

✳ let's choreograph in colour

Here is the opportunity to put movement, sight and sound together ~ the kinetic, the visual, and the auditory — VERY SIMPLE!

- Listen to a piece of colourful music, e.g. "Can Can" by Rossini. Imagine a Dance Hall scene. Ask the students what colours they can see in their "minds' eyes". Bright? Dull? Hot? Cold? Variety? Select a group to "choreograph" movement using coloured pieces of cloth, scarves, or streamers ~ rather like a cheer squad at a sporting event. Perhaps you could give them an idea of the can-can chorus line with a high kick?

Match movement with colours.

SUGGESTED PIECES ~ Make your own tape of music with "colourful" movement.

"Anitra's Dance" by Grieg — Colours: pinks, purples, blues?...exotic Eastern colours... weaving, graceful

"Ballet of the Unhatched Chicks" by Moussorgsky — Colours: very light pastel colours and silver?... whimsical, streaky

"Circus Music" by Copland — Colours: bright yellows, bright purples, reds, greens, a few sawdusty colours?... garish, raucous

"Dance of the Sugar Plum Fairy" by Tchaikovsky — Colours: pinks, blues, cream, silver, gold, white?... delicate, light

"Pantomime" by Kabalevsky — Colours: browns, blacks, greys, dark blues?... sombre, heavy

N.B. See TEXTURE, p. 48, re source of suggested music pieces.

LISTENING TO COLOUR

❋ match music with paintings

To match music with paintings, there needs to be a common quality in both. Is the music soft and gentle? Is the painting soft and gentle? The colours in the painting will give the strongest clues to its overall quality. The content will also affect its overall quality. So listen to the music, decide on its overall quality, then look for a painting with the same quality. In the pairs below, qualities such as quietness, loneliness, dithery-ness, active-ness, heaviness and gracefulness can be seen and heard.

THE MUSIC	THE PAINTING
● "Berceuse" by Stravinsky............ [From "The Firebird Suite"]	"The Lost Child" by Fred McCubbin [Aust.] or "The Tragedy" by Pablo Picasso [Spain]
● "Twittering Machine" by Schuller......	"The Twittering Machine" by Paul Klee [Swiss] or "Blue Poles" by Jackson Pollock [Am.]
FOR HUMOUR, TRY......	
● "Dagger Dance" by Herbert.........	"Five O'clock, Collins Street" by John Brack [Aust.]
● "Can Can" by Rossini...............	"Spirit of the Plains" by Sydney Long [Aust.]
● "From the Diary of a Fly" by Bartok...	"Down on his Luck" by Fred McCubbin [Aust.]

The songs below are from the Australian Broadcasting Commission's song books printed each year to accompany school music broadcasts —

"Mixing Colours" by L. Milne – "SING TOGETHER!" 1982
"Sing a Rainbow" by A. Hamilton – "SING ALONG" 1983
"Rainbow Snake" by R. McPherson – "SING ALONG" 1983

N.B. See TEXTURE, p. 48, re source of suggested music pieces.

WRITING ABOUT COLOUR

❋ let's add colour to our words

IMPORTANT! Try to saturate the students with interest in colour before asking them to write about it. The following exercise is a starting point.

● Give each student a square [approx 15cm²] of yellow, blue and red cellophane. Look around the room through each colour and with one colour superimposed over another to see the colour "mixes". Now venture outside and see the trees in blue and the clouds in green ... See Activity 23, p. 40.

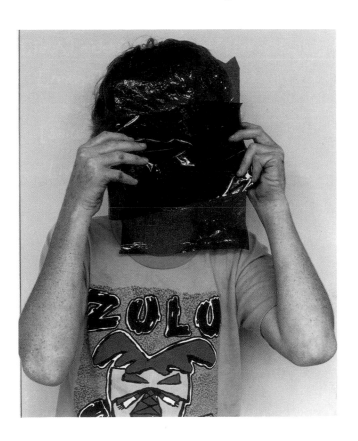

a) Find some colour **similes** ... "as red as a rose", "as grey as a ghost". Make up some of your own ... "as red as a rooster in a rotisserie", "as blue as a blow-fly in an ice-cube", "brown as a farmer's boot" ~ "night, like a black coat", "snow, like steaming white porridge".

b) Take these similes a step further for the older students ~ "night, like an undertaker", "snow, steaming like a winter's breakfast", or as **metaphors** "night, the undertaker", "ski-ing in porridge".

c) Students could write their own **fables**. "How the snow came to be white", "How the Crow Came to be Black", "How the Sink came to be Pink".

d) Make up **stories** that feature colour. Check through the colour-intense subjects on the page opposite to start ideas flowing. These stories would lend themselves well to illustration in colour. This would also be a good opportunity for the students to study techniques of colour illustration in books.

poetry — WRITING ABOUT COLOUR

e)   Have an **anthology search** to find phrases or lines in which the poet has used colour words or colour-intense imagery. Try "My Country" by Dorothea McKellar [Aust.], "Bellbirds" by Henry Kendall [Aust.] and poems by Dylan Thomas [Welsh] and Gerard Manly Hopkins [Eng.]. Check anthologies first before expecting children to wade through volumes, finding nothing. The Librarian will help.

f)   Make up **poems** with each line starting with a colour, or a **haiku** about colour. Find some books of haiku. All these could be used with displays.

g)   Make up some **rhyming couplets** [Find some by Alexander Pope, the English poet.] The children can relate these easily to their own world ~

> When I eat stew,
> I turn a bright hue.

> Colours sailing against the light,
> The wind has blown away my kite.

Here are some colour-intense **SUBJECTS** for writing and painting.

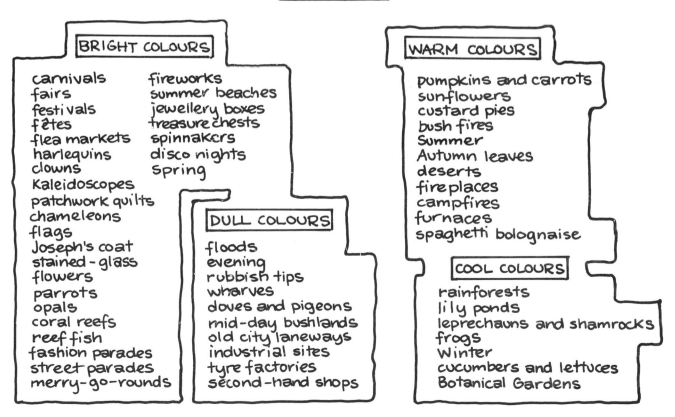

BRIGHT COLOURS

carnivals
fairs
festivals
fêtes
flea markets
harlequins
clowns
kaleidoscopes
patchwork quilts
chameleons
flags
Joseph's coat
stained-glass
flowers
parrots
opals
coral reefs
reef fish
fashion parades
street parades
merry-go-rounds

fireworks
summer beaches
jewellery boxes
treasure chests
spinnakers
disco nights
spring

DULL COLOURS

floods
evening
rubbish tips
wharves
doves and pigeons
mid-day bushlands
old city laneways
industrial sites
tyre factories
second-hand shops

WARM COLOURS

pumpkins and carrots
sunflowers
custard pies
bush fires
summer
Autumn leaves
deserts
fireplaces
campfires
furnaces
spaghetti bolognaise

COOL COLOURS

rainforests
lily ponds
leprechauns and shamrocks
frogs
winter
cucumbers and lettuces
Botanical Gardens

WRITING ABOUT COLOUR   scripts

h)   Show the students pictures of masks and costumes used by people of different ethnic groups ~ for carnivals, pagents, rituals, and so on. Study colours and patterns of primitive African jewellery and head-gear. What masks were used for ancient Greek drama choruses? What do the Mud Men of Papua New Guinea look like? What would we wear to a Mardi Gras? Students can make simple **MASKS** or paint each other's faces. Now write the **script**, for a conversation between two people from different cultures.

Photograph (detail): Stuart Riley

Courtesy of the Courier-Mail, Brisbane

These children from the Kuku Yalanji tribe are performing a corroboree as part of a project run by the Mossman Gorge Community Council in North Queensland.

i)   Select a legend or story from another culture. Write a **script** for your own version as a play. The students could design sets or costumes in appropriate colours. At right is an Indonesian costume seen at Expo '88, Brisbane, and a Balinese dancer. Quite often families from other cultures will lend ethnic costumes, proudly, for class activities.

COLLECTION AND DISPLAY OF WORDS

✳ This is a `BIG` MOMENT ~ a tally of the vocabulary that has been collected so far.

LET'S CHECK AND ORGANISE A
READY-REFERENCE BANK
FOR THE FUTURE

Collect all the words and good phrases USED, HEARD or SEEN and add any more you wish from

- your collected list
- a dictionary
- the Art program
- a thesaurus

OR memory

BEST IDEA...If you haven't already done so, put these words onto WORD CARDS for future resources, displays, and so on.

SEE NEXT PAGE.

DISPLAY ALL THE WORDS AND GOOD PHRASES FOR THE CLASS TO SEE.

©

COLLECTION AND DISPLAY OF WORDS

some words related to colour

hue
tint
shade
neutralized
greyed
intensity
value
tone
pure
bright
dull
cool
hot
warm
cold
dark
light
graded
variegated

monochromatic
neighbouring
adjacent
analogous
contrasting
complementary
harmonious
discordant

Primary
Secondary
Tertiary

pale
soft
fresh
bold
loud
clashing
gaudy
riotous
festive
garish
harsh
flamboyant
hard

like a . . .
carnival
raw steak
custard

clean
vivid
glossy
matt
lustrous
iridescent
burnished
raw
opalescent
luminous
opaque
transparent
faded
strong
weak
plain
deep
intense
shimmering
dazzling
brilliant
radiant
sparkling
glowing

glorious
sunny
fiery
lucid
scintillating
wishy-washy
showy
eerie
melting
quiet
rich
delicate
fragile
dreary
drab
striking
startling
sombre
murky
subtle
wan
sickly
pallid
shrieking
florid
muted
mellow
ashen
anaemic

metallic
rusty
earthy
electric
nocturnal
dusky
pastel
kaleidoscopic
emphatic
lively

gentle
royal
feminine
imposing
insipid
depressing
oppressive
aggressive
violent
threatening
sinister
foreboding
mundane
hypnotic
happy

like . . .
mulberries
canaries
parrots
Arabian Nights

SECTION TWO

Practical experiences

Rainbows can be a serious concern.

Seeing the world in a new light.

- <u>EXPERIENCE IN THE MOST SUITABLE MEDIUM</u> ~ <u>PAINT</u>
  - EXPERIMENTAL "PLAY"
  - DIRECTED EXPERIENCE
  - APPLIED EXPERIENCE
  - COLOUR STUDY - painting ; roller prints
- <u>OTHER MEDIA AND TECHNIQUES</u>: dyeing ; cellophane collage ; "stained-glass" collage ; paper collage ; painting [a note about painting] ; puppets
- <u>"DOING YOUR OWN THING" TIME</u>

EXPERIMENTAL "PLAY"　　　　painting

Paint.... colours, colours, colours

THIS IS AN IMPORTANT LEARNING SESSION! DON'T MISS IT EVEN IF YOU KNOW THE CLASS IS PROFICIENT IN HANDLING PAINT.

Join up sheets of cartridge paper or other suitable paper to make one long sheet, on tables pushed together to make one long bench. Put painting materials [see TEACHER'S GUIDE, p.62] in centre, with students working from either side. Put only RED, YELLOW and BLUE paint in containers. Tell students they are not painting pictures ~ just having fun mixing paint on their palettes [icecream lids will do], and covering the whole of the paper with as many **different** colours as they can mix ~ leaving no areas of white paper. Use the frieze later to decorate the room.

- Use the widest brushes, e.g. the "varnish brushes" and watch to see that studen don't use them like pestles. Encourage a stroking action, to preserve bristles.

- Watch for students adding too much water to the paint so it becomes transpare all the time. Use the water for cleaning brushes before using another colour. Excess colour on brushes can be wiped back onto the paint tray.

- If some students simply go over and over an area, turning the colour to "mud ~ so be it. They learn that that is what happens. But, do show them the way colours mix to make new colours. Praise anyone who discovers a colour mix. share the discovery.

exploring techniques DIRECTED EXPERIENCE

Assist the class to explore different techniques of applying paint. "Anything goes." Artists use all of the following. The students will discover more. Join in the exploring and don't be frightened to demonstrate. Try rollers, sponges, tea-bags...

RESIST and WET INTO WET:

Draw heavily with Craypas or crayon, then wash over the top with very watery paint, blobbing in other colours, also watery, so the colours run together. The oily crayon resists the watery paint. Use a large brush.

THE BLOB AND DRIBBLE:

Blob very watery paint at the top of the page, hold it up vertically, and let the paint run down. If desired, keep introducing new colours to run down over the top. This has made the very romantic bushland scene below.

YEAR 4

YEAR 7

DIRECTED EXPERIENCE   exploring techniques

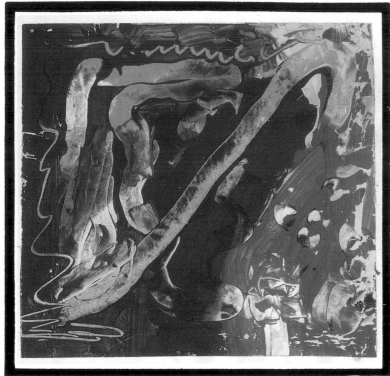

YEAR 2

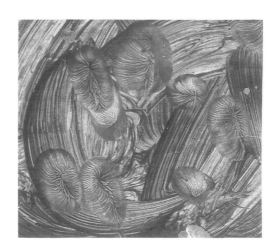

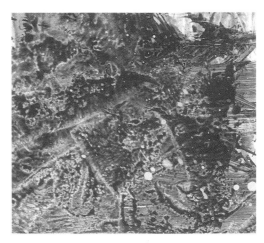

SGRAFFITO: Cover paper with thick Craypas. Paint over thickly and scrape into while wet. [Top left]

GLAZING: Rub paint into paper with rag/tissue. Rub in other colours over the top. [Some papers are too asorbant or glossy.] [Above]

PRINTING: Press fingers or object into paint. [Top right]

PRINTING with paint on rag/tissue. [centre right]

SCRAPING with other end of brush into paint, and

SPATTERING paint from stiff bristles. [Right]

painting   APPLIED EXPERIENCE

NOW LET'S APPLY DIFFERENT TECHNIQUES to a subject. See p. 27 for ideas.

YEAR 4

In the painting above, you will discover scraping, spattering, dribbling, glazing, [on _too_ smooth a paper], printing with the side of a flat brush, fingers and a tissue ... there are no ordinary brush strokes. Quite an exciting piece of work!

A COLOUR WHEEL

Students of every Year level can cope with colour study knowledge, if it is presented as <u>LANGUAGE TO ACCOMPANY ACTIVITY</u>. If the students find some terms or concepts difficult, don't labour the point ~ leave it for later, another year perhaps. Just ensure they can manage the associated practical work.

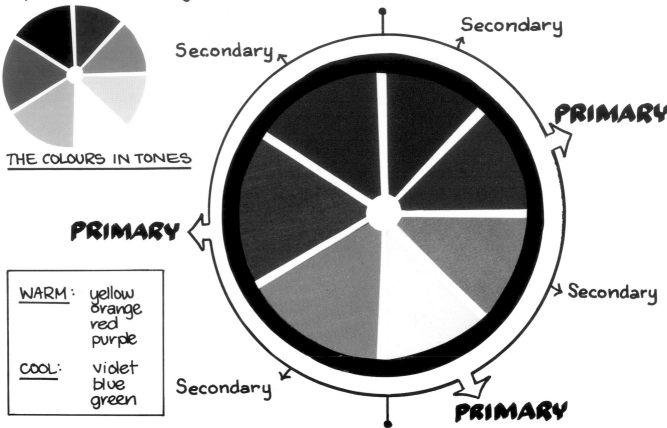

THE COLOURS IN TONES

Secondary

Secondary

PRIMARY

PRIMARY

Secondary

Secondary

PRIMARY

<u>WARM</u>: yellow
orange
red
purple

<u>COOL</u>: violet
blue
green

ALL THE COLOURS ON THE WHEEL ARE <u>**HUES**</u>, colours at their <u>brightest</u>, their highest intensity. Take the Primaries straight from the Chromacryl containers. Mix these to make the Secondary colours. Paint each colour separately. Cut into wedges and assemble the wheel.

a) **Paint** a huge colour wheel, or several small ones, and attach to the ceiling or high on a wall, for ready reference.

b) Everyone loves to paint **rainbows!** The colour wheel is just a segment of the rainbow bent around. Don't worry about the correct order of colours for young children.

A segment of the spectrum

roller prints   COLOUR MIXING

The aim is to experience colour mixing of **PRIMARY** colours to produce
SECONDARY colours, using a visually exciting technique. See p.2 for the
colour mixes. **TERTIARY** colours will result from the mixture of all <u>three</u>
Primary colours. If you haven't any rollers, just mix paint with brushes.

<u>SET UP FOUR "STATIONS"</u> in the room. If the tabletops are not made of laminex
or similar non-absorbent material, then tape down a rectangle of strong clear or
black plastic, approx. 30 x 24 cms [If clear plastic is used, put white paper underneath.] If tabletop is laminex, paint can be put directly onto it. See centre photograph, TEACHER'S GUIDE, p. 63.

AT STATION 1 put RED and BLUE only onto flat paint tray

2 put RED and YELLOW " " " " "

3 put BLUE and YELLOW " " " " "

4 put BLUE and YELLOW and RED " " "

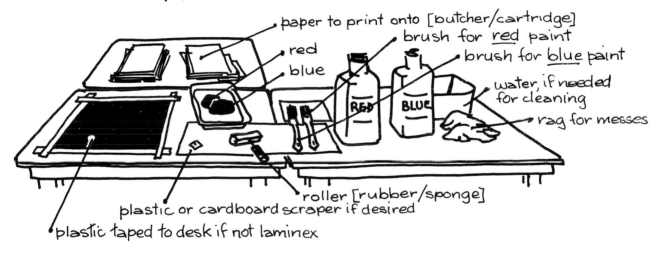

- paper to print onto [butcher/cartridge]
- red
- blue
- brush for <u>red</u> paint
- brush for <u>blue</u> paint
- water, if needed for cleaning
- rag for messes
- roller [rubber/sponge]
- plastic or cardboard scraper if desired
- plastic taped to desk if not laminex

Divide class into four groups, one at each station. Rotate these when all the
students have had a turn making the roller prints. No particular patterns are
required. JUST OBSERVE THE COLOUR MIXES!

1. Apply paint to roller with brushes.

2. Roll paint onto plastic or desk-top and scrape a pattern into it. note colour mixes

3. Press paper onto paint then lift off, i.e., "pull a print". roll down

COLOUR MIXING   monochromatic colour scheme

The aim is to experience mixing **tints, shades** and **greyed** colours to make **MONOCHROMATIC** colour schemes. [MONO :one alone, CHROMA : colour]

The class can work in two groups, one using reds and one using blues. Set the paint out as below on palettes or trays, one between two students.

Polystyrene food tray →

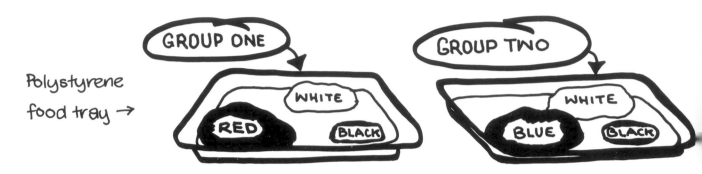

GROUP ONE   WHITE   RED   BLACK

GROUP TWO   WHITE   BLUE   BLACK

<u>N.B.</u> When yellow acrylic paint is mixed with black, chemical reactions cause it to turn green rather than dark yellow, as in yellow ochre. Because of this, it is better to omit it from this activity. This could be explained to the students.

YEAR 4

SHOW STUDENTS HOW TO MIX

PAINT..."Mix a little of this with a little of that on the palette, paint it on, scrape any extra back onto the palette, wash the brush in water, dab it on the rag, and start again."

TINT . . . . . HUE + WHITE

SHADE . . . HUE + BLACK [a <u>little</u>]

GREYED. . . HUE + GREY [black + white]

So, if using <u>RED</u> . . . RED, PINKS, MAROONS, MURKY PINKS AND MURKY MAROONS, with BLACK, WHITE, GREYS = a MONO—CHROMATIC COLOUR SCHEME. If painting a picture rather than a design, here are some suggested subject starters : <u>BLUES</u> : rainy day, storm, surfing, under-water, dream, remembering. <u>REDS</u> : desert, bush-fire, heat-wave, fire-works, Mars landscape, fear.

DYEING

This need not be an expensive activity. However, if commercial dyes and plenty of plain cloth such as calico are available, then the finished product could be of a more permanent nature, eg. classroom curtains. Many books are available on tie-dying which is a suitable technique. Look in the Library.

- Dyeing is simply "dunking in colour". Instead of expensive dyes, try food colouring + water ; powder paint + water ; or just Chromacryl + water. And to continue learning about colour mixing, start with the three Primaries. These will become mixed in the containers as the students work, so be prepared to set up some fresh containers as well.

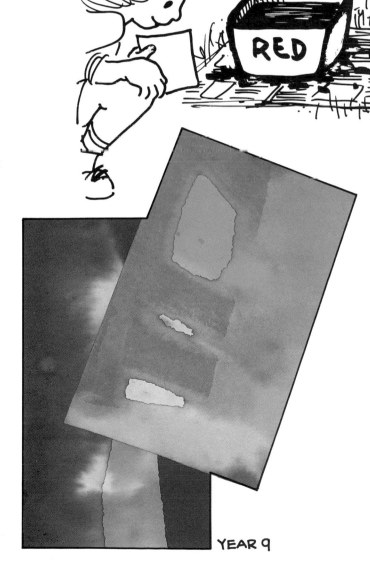

YEAR 9

Dunk pieces of butcher's paper into different colours—just corners or sides until the paper is covered. Let some dry before dunking again so edges are made. Peg them onto a fence or line. Later use them for ink drawings, or cut up for collage or construction.

CELLOPHANE COLLAGE

This activity is a good introduction to colour mixing.

Have a FUN SESSION first — looking at the world, indoors and outdoors, through different coloured cellophane. Each student needs at least one square of each colour, dark RED, YELLOW and dark BLUE.

Direct students towards discovering that yellow over blue shows green, yellow over red shows orange, etc.

[If the red is too weak, use two layers each time.] MAKE SOME SPECIAL "GLASSES" IF YOU WISH.

● To make the cellophane collage, spread several metres of clear plastic on tables pushed together. Place white paper underneath so that the colours are clear. Have the cellophane cut into shapes, any size. With clear adhesive, tape these down onto the plastic, layer over layer, colour over colour. [Help the younger children.] Hang the work against a window, or over some structure so that it serves as a "roof". Some students may have the opportunity to see Leonard French's stained glass ceiling at the Victorian Arts Centre.

PAPER COLLAGE

24 "stained-glass' collage

Cut some black plastic into 4 strips each ½ metre wide. Show students how to cut holes in it by folding and cutting into the fold. Sticky-tape pieces of red, yellow and blue cellophane over the holes, overlapping to produce multi-colours. Any paper, any size, will do if black plastic is not available.

Class can work in four groups ~ one strip each.

Hang the works against a strong light or with white paper behind them.

25 paper collage

Go on a **COLOUR SPREE!** Cut abstract shapes out of coloured paper and glue them onto a square of backing paper. Black is a good background colour. Each child's square could then be joined to another to make one large "happy wall", perhaps for the Administration Block to balance up all those sporting trophies! The collage could be used to teach MONOCHROMATIC, NEIGHBOURING and CONTRASTING colour schemes. See p. 3, and the colour wheel on p. 36. What type of scheme did each student use?

PAINTED OBJECTS

tins

lids

Paint anything!

sticks

old shoes

leaves

blocks of wood

Year 2

stones

Paint the teacher !? [This book is for teachers only.]

...boxes, old book-covers, old T-shirts, hand-bags, vases, tins with labels, lids...

A butcher paper table-cloth for the teacher, or someone's birthday.

Paint the windows. Chromacryl comes off easily.

Have a "white elephant" collection of discarded objects from home. Paint the suitable ones ~ perhaps sell them to raise funds for more paint or use them to brighten up some dull area around the school.

Try a group activity. At left, a Year 2 class is working on a frieze for the Music Room, painting "dragon music" and learning the shapes of notes at the same time. They are also imbuing their concepts of musical notation with colour and pleasurable associations.

a note about painting

Painting is usually the activity closest related to the image of "being an artist". It is probably the most personal of all the student's Art works, so the one to which they are most sensitive. So, it is in this area that they can be most discouraged, even "destroyed", for the rest of their lives — or encouraged and fulfilled. The teacher, as commentator, has a responsibility not to belittle, deflate, tease or chastise, as the consequences can be permanently damaging — and UNSEEN. [This is not referring to chastisement for bad behaviour during Art sessions, of course.] It is during the painting session a student often becomes categorized forever as "specially-gifted" or "hopeless", either quite erroneously. So take care — be encouraging.

PUPPETS
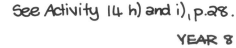

• hand-held masks

- Cut cardboard shape and staple to ruler
- Paint a nose or glue on any knobbly object
- Simply hold a cloth
- Match colour with character

[Let students use their own ideas — stencils drawn up by adults are the curse of creativity!]

See Activity 14 h) and i), p.28.

YEAR 8

• sock puppets
Simply glue on cloth eyes. If the class can sew, cut along the toe line and sew in an oval of cloth ~ a tongue also, if desired ~ as in the photograph above. Let the students invent their own so <u>each one is different</u>.

• paper bag puppets
Stuff a paper bag with crumpled paper and tie it together at the neck. Paint the face, glue on wool, streamers, cloth and so on. Paper bags provide their own "built-in" ears for all sorts of animals. LET EVERY PUPPET BE CREATED BY THE STUDENT'S <u>OWN</u> INGENUITY — NOT MASS PRODUCTION FROM STERILE INSTRUCTIONS!

Photographer: Charles Zuber

Courtesy of Pat Zuber, Queensland

At left, are puppets made by Pat Zuber, tutor for the Queensland Arts Council. Such organizations can arrange visits, even to remote areas, and provide professional expertise and excitement never to be forgotten!

AND...

"DOING YOUR OWN thing" TIME

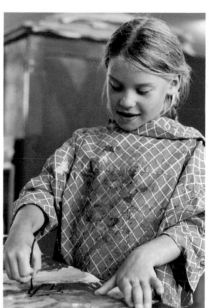

Give... as many opportunities as possible for the students to select their **own subjects**, their **own media and techniques**, ranging from drawing realistically from life to pure abstraction, and their **own time limits** ~ perhaps in short sessions over several days ~ time to work on one piece. It is important to **praise and encourage all** subject choices and styles, to ensure students do not select according to approval only.

For colour-orientated subjects for painting, see p. 27 to start ideas flowing.

For a major individual "do your own thing" activity, see p. 46.

a wall of one's own

An opportunity of a life-time for Billy ~ a living Chromacryl kid!
There is no reason why this should not be a common occurrence.

Evaluation

OBSERVE the student at work ~ to assess confidence, self-reliance, application of knowledge, manipulative skills, work habits, and so on.

"ARE YOU HAPPY WITH WHAT YOU HAVE DONE, ALLISON?"

DOES THE STUDENT NEED HELP?

TALK to the student ~ establish the intentions and compare with results. Was the selection of medium, technique and types of colours suitable for the subject? Were the intentions directed toward the REALISTIC RECORD, the EXPERIMENTAL, INTELLECTUAL, IMAGINATIVE, DECORATIVE, AESTHETIC, or as a PERSONAL EXPRESSION — or as PRACTICE? See pp. 48-55.

"WHAT IS IT ABOUT, CHLOE?" "WHY DID YOU USE THOSE COLOURS, LYN?"

LOOK at the student's work in relation to all experiences covered so far. Has knowledge been applied? TAKE THE WORK HOME. GIVE IT A GOOD "SEEING" — READ IT AS IF IT WAS WRITTEN TO YOU, PERSONALLY. Every mark a student makes means something, so don't miss it.

COMPARE the student's work with previous work. Is he or she trying new things or simply repeating "successful" formulae?

See EVALUATION section in TEACHER'S GUIDE, pp. 57-59.

What to look for—

DON'T FORGET
TO CONSIDER
TEMPERAMENTS.
Each student has
an individual style.
See TEACHER'S
GUIDE, pp. 50-55.

REALISTIC RECORD

This painting shows the child has learned to apply her knowledge of colour mixing, observing the colours from life, although using only yellow, blue and black. She has also overcome her fear of painting in the background and going over edges already drawn in. She has made good use of her experience in mixing hues, tints and shades [Activity 21, p. 38]. This painting came from Activity 8a), p. 20.

Amanda   YEAR 4

Trevor YEAR 4

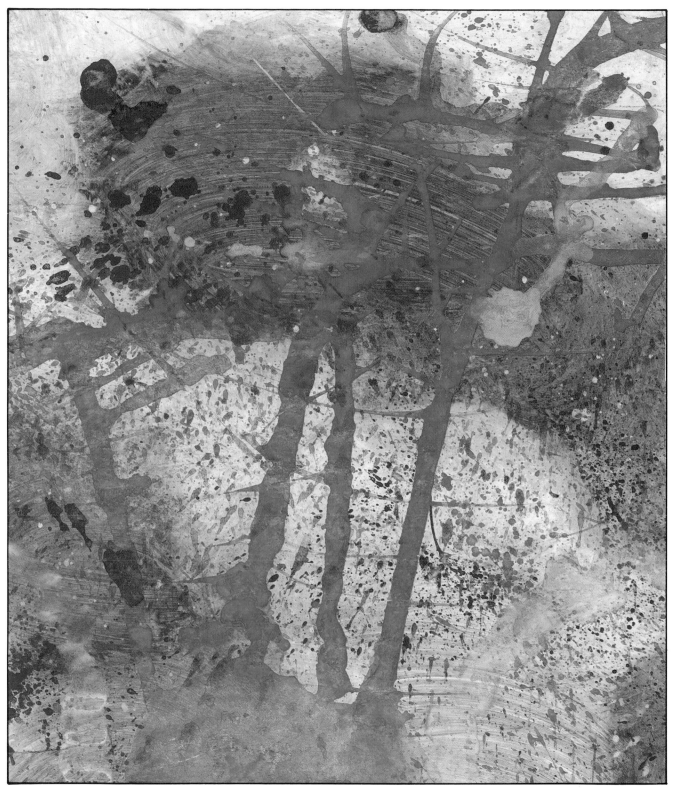

This interesting work from Activity 18, p. 35, shows the child has applied himself to the task of experimenting freely. It can be seen quite easily as a finished piece of work now it has been cut from the page and given neat edges. Keep an eye open for such "little gems" and mount them for the classroom wall. It helps students take their experimental work seriously.

INTELLECTUAL

Chanel YEAR 10

Martin YEAR 5

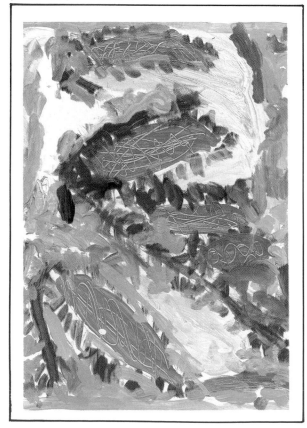

Both these samples came from the study of warm colours. See p. 36.

In the computer print-out above, the image was based on a drawing from life in the schoolyard. Notice how dots of different colours affect the colour of larger areas for the better.

In the painting at left, however, the colours had to be mixed ~ a harder task, particularly since it was painted from life. Changing colours from real life can be an aesthetically illuminating experience, as the painting quite often looks better than the original subject.

John YEAR 7

This sgraffito painting depicts what the child would have liked in his backyard — a ferris-wheel and friends. It is direct and uses the picture space to communicate exactly the items of his wish. However, it is more than the "grocery-list" type of picture. The colours and quality of linework are SUITABLE for his imagined idea ～ carnival colours, exciting and lively. The additional circles show his awareness of space in his composition.

DECORATIVE

Alan YEAR 5

This piece of work is interesting because the child took a decorative approach to a painting-from-life subject, re-arranging the plant form and repeating a spiralling tendril to give a patterned effect. He has also chosen appropriate colours for his task at hand ~ a contrasting colour scheme. Compare this painting with those on pages 48 and 50 done during the same session. All the students selected plant forms from a class collection, with the teacher suggesting they choose a warm or cool, a monochromatic, neighbouring or contrasting colour scheme. [see pages 36 and 3.] All the three students have taken different approaches ~ realistic; intellectual but free in application of paint; and decorative. This is something to aim for in a painting session ~ to have children developing their **OWN** approaches as well as learning or consolidating knowledge or technical skill.

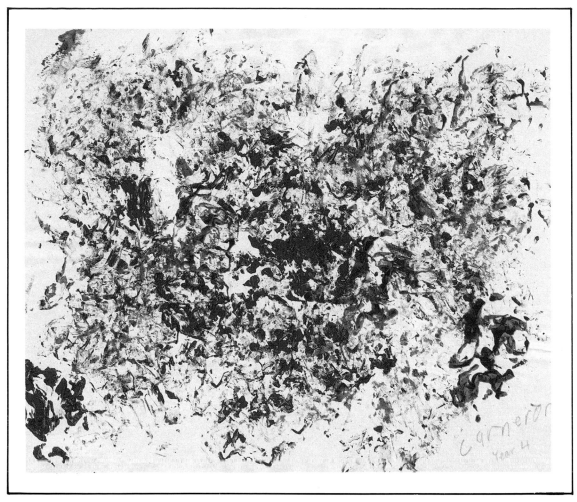

Cameron YEAR 4

This work is a case of a student discovering an effective technique while experimenting [Activity 17, pp. 33, 34] and following it up in a "Doing your own thing" session. The effect of dabbling paint lightly over the paper with the corner of a rag, first one colour, then the other, appealed to him aesthetically so he completed quite a large surface in just this one technique, all to his own liking. The technique has been kept fresh and consistent throughout [which isn't as easy as it looks], and the whole surface has a convincing life of its own.

PERSONAL EXPRESSION

Diane YEAR I

"When I grow up, I'm going to be a lady." This beautiful, spontaneous painting, although very simple, makes a direct, strong statement. "This will be me with long, flowing hair." Notice the flower petals around the head. The direct brush-strokes are completely in keeping with the direct statement, which is characteristic of young children's work. Teachers need to nurture this characteristic or it will be lost, mainly through outside pressure for the child to produce the neat, colouring-in type of "proper picture"! This "proper picture" is a manifestation of biassed ignorance that is very destructive.

Melissa YEAR 7

The painting above was done as practice in mixing colours ~ blue and yellow to make green, and then making tints, shades, and greyed colours. The child could choose any subject, any technique, any approach. The colour mixing is very good, although the figures could have been made clearer with more contrast in tone [see p.16]. This would have been easier to do if this stage of the painting had dried, so a follow-up session would have been beneficial. There has been one little adventure into interesting technique with the scraping into the paint in the foreground. The subject matter is clear enough ~ a football team on field ~ a handsome crew, and an interesting subject for Melissa, Year 7, to choose!

A group project with Chromacryl, on a discarded blackboard.

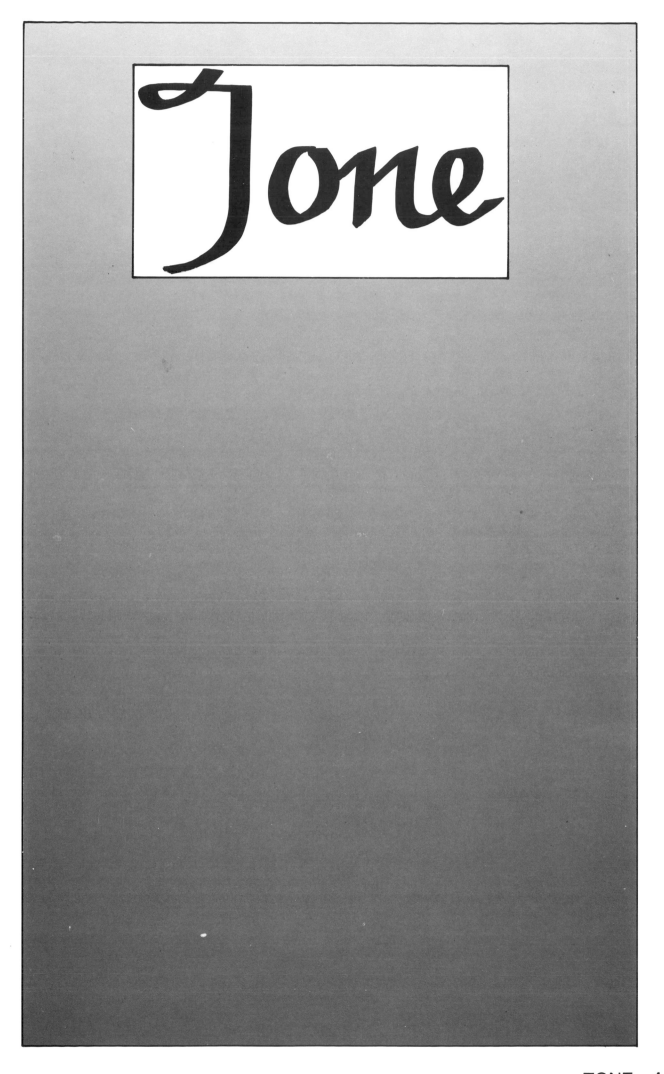

Tone

Come, stand in stark defiance of our vulnerability, black against the light of suns, and cast a long, yet longer shadow across the hills of morning. Or wait, below the clatter of the darks and lights of flying birds, until the mid-day silence bids our eyes to close against the glare. And then, come wander into darkening valleys ~ darker, until we are engulfed in dreams. And we will keep the harmony of night by moving only on the edges of the moon.

Contents

Photograph opposite: Auda McClean, Baralaba, Queensland.

TONE IS . . . the degree of LIGHTNESS or DARKNESS of a colour.

N.B. Take care not to confuse TONE with INTENSITY. Both are aspects of colour and have been dealt with in the COLOUR Unit. The decision to make a separate unit for TONE in this program, stems from the fact that it is not promoted in this society's every-day life. However it is very important in the world of black and white media, e.g. the newspaper, which is part of our society's every day life. Actually, it is important in all things visual.

PHYSICAL TYPES OF TONE

| LIGHT | MEDIUM | DARK |

See also, the "natural order" of colours, COLOUR, p. 3.

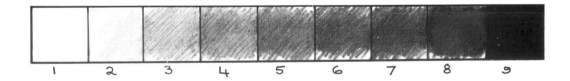

| 1 | 2 | 3 | 4 | 5 | 6 | 7 | 8 | 9 |

A 9-TONE SCALE ~ white is TONE^1; black is TONE^9; all other colours fall somewhere in between, e.g. RED^8 would be a very dark maroon, RED^2 would be a very light pink. These types of scales are used in the commercial world to describe dyes, printers' inks, and so on.

GRADED

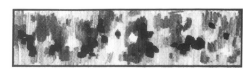

VARIEGATED

Read page 2. It is the POET'S FORM OF THE DIAGRAMS ABOVE!

SUGGESTED WORK PLAN FOR A BLOCK UNIT OF 5 WEEKS ON TONE

Mix 'n' match your own activities if not following the plan below. Be flexible!
Omit or extend activities where desired or practical. See N.B. in LINE, p.5.

WEEK ONE

AWARENESS:	Seeing tone –	ACTIVITY 1...p.8. Seeing Safari
		ACTIVITY 7·23...pp.15·31. Drawing from life
PRACTICAL:	Experimental "play" –	ACTIVITY 16...p.24. Painting
		ACTIVITY 17...p.25. Wall chart discussion

WEEK TWO

AWARENESS:	Seeing tone –	ACTIVITY 2...p.9·10. Audio-visuals. Display
PRACTICAL:	Directed experience–	ACTIVITY 18...pp.26·27. Charcoal techniques
	Applied experience –	ACTIVITY 19...p.28. Charcoal drawing

WEEK THREE

AWARENESS:	Seeing tone –	ACTIVITY 3...p.11. Appreciation [Student's Book]
		ACTIVITY 4...p.12. Cartoon strips
		ACTIVITY 6...p.14. Tone display
PRACTICAL:	Other media –	ACTIVITY 20·21...pp.29·30. Pencil techniques
		ACTIVITY 22...p.30. Unity through tone
		ACTIVITY 5...p.13. Tones in composition

WEEK FOUR

AWARENESS:	Integration –	ACTIVITY 8...p.16. Drama and dance
		ACTIVITY 11...p.18 Listening to tone in music
		ACTIVITY 12...p.19. Tone with instruments
PRACTICAL:	Other media –	ACTIVITY 24·25·26...p.32. Working with paper

WEEK FIVE

AWARENESS:	Integration –	ACTIVITY 9·10...p.17. Movement · Video shoot
		ACTIVITY 13...p.19. Writing about tone
		ACTIVITY 14...p.20. Computer Graphics
	Language of tone –	ACTIVITY 15...pp.21·22. Word display
PRACTICAL:	Some tone study –	ACTIVITY 27·28...pp.33·35. Depth and 3D
		ACTIVITY 29...p.36. "Doing your own thing" time

N.B. Remember that **AWARENESS EXPERIENCES** are to work hand in hand with **PRACTICAL EXPERIENCES** so that students have a source for ideas.

Materials

THE BASIC KIT   – double if possible

CHROMACRYL PAINT – black, white, red/blue* ... pp. 13·24·31

CHARCOAL – 3 boxes – block, compressed ... pp. 17·26-28·31·33

COLOURED PAPER – ½ pkt matt squares – 254mm² ... p. 32

GLUE – [powdered] → ¼ litre ... p. 32

    Also, if possible ~   PASTELS – 4 boxes ... p. 31

                        INK ... 1 btle ... p. 31

THE BARE BONES KIT

CHROMACRYL PAINT – black, white, red/blue* ... pp. 24·31

CHARCOAL – 3 boxes – block compressed ... pp. 17·26-28·31

    Also, if possible ~ COLOURED PAPER – ½ pkt matt squares

                   254²mm / ordinary brown paper and

                   black cover paper ... p. 32

                   PASTELS – 4 boxes ... p. 31

                   INK – 1 btle black ... p. 31

    Make your own ~ FLOUR and WATER GLUE ... p. 32

THE *running on* ... . THIN AIR KIT

CHROMACRYL PAINT – black, white, red/blue* ... pp. 24·31

Scavenge, save, and make your own, as for above kits.

FOR ALL KITS: Collection of pieces of cloth, clothing, objects, magazine

                   cuttings in black, white and greys ~ and in monochromatic

                   colours, e.g. light blues, pure blue, dark blues.

* Commercial Names : Cool Yellow, Warm Red, Warm Blue, Black, White.

SECTION ONE

Awareness experiences

AIMS:
- to awaken an interest in tone **for its own sake**
- to develop a **vocabulary** about tone at all levels of awareness ~ physical to abstract

- SEEING TONE
- INTEGRATED EXPERIENCES WITH TONE
- LANGUAGE OF TONE

THE SEEING SAFARI

AIMS: • to help the students learn to `SEE`, i.e. to see **more** than mere physical presence of objects
• to develop further a **VOCABULARY** about tone on all levels of awareness ~ physical to abstract

Start in the classroom, finding what tones the room is "made of". Which is the darkest, which is the lightest object in sight? Which parts are the <u>same</u> in degree of darkness and lightness? Look through squinted eyes to take the intensity of the colour out. Imagine the scene as a **black and white photograph**. Which objects would be mid-grey? Now, venture out into the schoolyard. Point out things of **LIGHT** TONE, **DARK** TONE, **GRADED** TONE [changing gradually from dark to light], **VARIEGATED** TONE [mottled darks and lights], **CONTRAST** of TONE [both very dark and very light], and **HARMONY** of TONE [similar in tones]. **COLLECT WORDS** used and put onto WORD CARDS. See pp. 21, 22.

Camera ready to collect resources?

"This is a motley crew."

"who can see tones that go from dark to light?" [graded]

"Which is the darkest one?"

Where are some contrasting tones?

"This one is light all over"

"It's spooky!"

Looking through blue cellophane helps to cut out much of the colour, making the scene much closer to a black and white photograph. Give each student a 15cm square and fold double.

When the students are seeing the physical types of tones, move into the more abstract, expressive vocabulary . . . . . . [see p.4 for physical types.]

gloomy . . . shadowy . . . startling . . . lively . . . glary . . . threatening . . . subtle . . . stark tones

MAKING THE MOST OF MEDIA

AUDIO-VISUAL RESOURCES:

Try some story-telling in B/W (black and white) on the overhead projector. Draw into a thin layer of sand in a shallow glass dish on the O.H.P. top. Add solid shapes into the sand. Try two projectors to superimpose images and to help sequence images. Legends are good subjects for stories.

Investigate sources of videos, films, strips, etc. about TONE, and/or make some yourself! Ask school and community Libraries, Education Centres, Film Centres, and so on.

Check the school television and radio broadcasts for Art programs. Timetables are usually available at the beginning of each year. Try to build up the school's resources as well as your own.

WATCH AND DISCUSS.

STATIC RESOURCES:

See next page.

LOOK AND DISCUSS.

DISPLAY in the classroom, or elsewhere in the school ~

- photographs you, or others, have taken
- pictures from magazines
- newspaper photographs
- posters
- record covers, book covers, and so on.

You may have space for only ONE photograph in your classroom ~ fine! It will have unrivalled status of importance ~ but do change it often.

MEDIA   classroom display

Compile a Class Photo Album with photographs of obvious types of tones. Use them in displays. Label and discuss them. The two photographs on this page feature dark, medium, light, graded and variegated tones. Both feature CONTRAST of tone, which produces their "strong presence" on the page. **Photocopy** photographs that are in colour and compare their tones in black and white. They can be enlarged and labels pinned or glued on them. Also, sections can be cut off so only the relevant sections are used for display.

APPRECIATION IN THE WORLD OF ART

DISCUSS the Art Works below in conjunction with the Student's Book, pp. 3, 5 and 13.

Collection of Coll Portley, Queensland

Tone is used to add weight to the design of this church of Notre Dame du Haut, France. Architect: Le Corbusier.

Bark painting by Narritjin Maymuru. Note how the areas of dark colour are spread perfectly throughout holding the whole story together.

Note the strong CONTRAST of tones [called MAJOR KEY] of the bark painting and the church. It makes them **definite** and **bold** The former tells a story of fish, crocodile and men, being turned into the Milky Way, the Southern Cross, and the two "pointers". The church is built like the **dramatic** head-dress of the nuns in that part of France. The Fairweather painting, however, is **quiet** and **soft**, with all

94.8 x 70.2 cm

Courtesy of the Tasmanian Museum and Art Gallery

"FLIGHT INTO EGYPT" by Ian FAIRWEATHER [1891–1974 AUST.] Acrylic on paper on hardboard. 1961.

parts intermingled **like a tapestry**. [It is in MINOR KEY because all the tones are similar.] The words in bold type can be added to WORD CARDS. See pp. 21, 22.

APPRECIATION IN THE STUDENT'S OWN WORLD

Collect some cartoon strips to study.

The newspaper cartoonist rarely has the opportunity to use colour, so TONE is important. As well as making each picture cleaver to look at, tones create ATMOSPHERE. Notice how the top strip is "calm" in tones; the second strip is active, with a variety of tones; the bottom one is dramatic and stark. These all fit the mood of the "story".

There may be murals on school walls or in the community. Discuss the pattern of tones in these. Look at them from a distance or through squinted eyes. Do they "carry" from a distance or do they become confused? Contrast of tones helps to keep them clear and eye-catching.

APPRECIATION OF TONE IN COMPOSITION

Collect some newspaper photographs to study.

The following is an interesting activity for Year 5 upwards. From newspapers, cut out photographs with STRONG CONTRASTS OF DARK AND LIGHT. Give one to each student along with a 2B or 4B pencil [or black paint], and some white chalk [or white paint]. Check to see if the chalk "takes" to the paper. Students shade in heavily, all the areas that are dark or darkish, so they are flat, black shapes. Blot out all details. Then go over the rest, the medium and lighter areas with white, blotting out all the details. What is left is a black and white **TONAL PATTERN**, very easy to see now that it is only in two tones. Tonal patterns are very important in pictures of all types ~ realistic or abstract ~ and extremely important in road signs and advertisements designed to be seen from a distance. A badly balanced or jumbled tonal pattern will produce a disturbing effect or illegibility. It is often the source of ~ "There's something wrong with my picture but I don't know what it is." See also, COLOUR, Activity 4, p. 16.

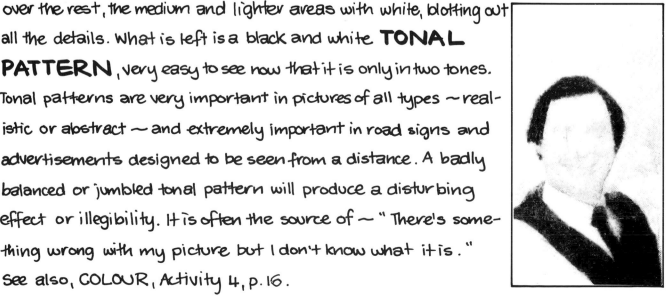

MAKING A TONE DISPLAY

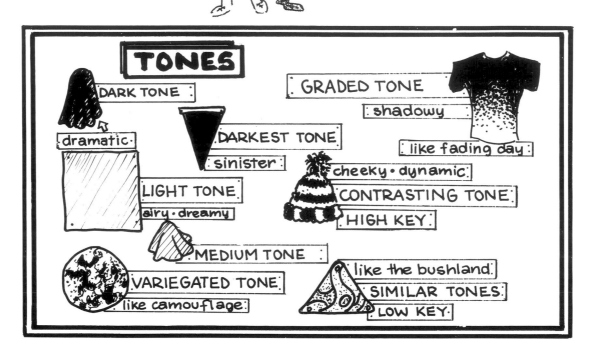

TONES ON CENTRE STAGE

TONES

DARK TONE

dramatic

DARKEST TONE

sinister

LIGHT TONE

airy · dreamy

MEDIUM TONE

VARIEGATED TONE

like camouflage

GRADED TONE

shadowy

like fading day

cheeky · dynamic

CONTRASTING TONE

HIGH KEY

like the bushland

SIMILAR TONES

LOW KEY

It is relatively easy to see tones when they are in black, greys or white. However, **venture into <u>coloured</u> objects in your display.** Be careful not to be affected by the brightness of the colour. Just imagine it in a black and white photograph. If some students, or teachers, cannot differentiate between colour and tone, don't worry ~ it will come later. It is probably the hardest of all concepts for the untrained eye, in the early stages of development.

[See also, the "natural order" of colours, COLOUR, p. 3.]

COLLECT ANY OBJECTS THAT CAN BE PINNED UP OR ARRANGED ON A TABLE. LABEL THEM WITH YOUR WORD CARDS.

DON'T FORGET THE ABSTRACT, EXPRESSIVE WORDS OR PHRASES...

e.g. dreary, vivid, aggressive, like shouting out, like the dying day...

RECORDING TONES FROM LIFE

See TEACHER'S GUIDE, pp. 22-27.

The easiest and most valuable lesson of all!

Take pencils and paper out into the school-yard. Find objects that are very **LIGHT**, very **DARK**, both very **LIGHT AND DARK** [contrasting], **GRADED** [from light into dark], or **VARIEGATED** [mottled with DARK and LIGHT]. Draw them as a collection of tones on the page. Don't worry about drawing in details. Just try to match the tones with those you see. Notice the parents in the photograph. "Running on Rainbows" has given them an opportunity to catch up on missed experiences.

Build up your resources. Show a student how to take a photograph. [Black and white film is less susceptible to disaster.]

DISPLAY EVERYONE'S WORK IF POSSIBLE.

Remember, when finding tone difficult to see, ask, "Is it light or dark? How would it look in a black and white photograph?"

◄ A student's page may look something like this.

TONE IN DRAMA AND DANCE

✳ let's move

a) Try some **drama** with the "SET-UP SITUATION and FREEZE" method ~

"Imagine you are in a DARK, DARK place."

"Freeze!"

"Now imagine a flood of BRIGHT LIGHT."

"Freeze!"

[A good time for photographs.]

Continue with situations of GRADED tones [light fading away or getting darker] and VARIEGATED tones [e.g. flashing disco lights]. Here students are able to act out reactions to tone in a dramatic context. <u>They are bringing to life the aesthetic qualities of the physical types of tone.</u>

b) Make up a short **play** or sequence in which the above light situations occur, e.g. "Midnight Visit to the Forest", "Underground City Adventure", "Lost in Caves".

c) Translate the above into **dance** with music from p.18. Dance segments from musicals or famous ballets on videos would help to show students that dance and drama work well together. Discuss the atmosphere of changing light on stage.

WATCHING TONE IN MOVEMENT

In a place made as dark as possible [perhaps under the school if not in a room], cover several students over with white or plain-coloured sheets, and turn them into ...

✳ slow moving sculptures

FREEZE AND OBSERVE

Try to arrange some strong light [natural, torch, projector, etc.] coming from one side only. Cover any light surfaces that might reflect light, with a dark cloth. If no dark area is available, use the ordinary classroom — it won't be as exciting but will be worth a try. The rest of the class can watch for tones — the darkest part of the "sculpture"; the lightest part; very dark edges up against very light edges [these are called **dynamic edges** because they attract the eye so powerfully]; graded tones from light to dark; harmony of similar tones, and so on. Drawing the "sculptures" in pencil [4B would be best, but 2B would do] or charcoal, would ensure the students were seeing the tones.

✳ video the above

Build up your resources for the future.
Try some **patterns** of tones —

For pattern — REPEAT, REPEAT, REPEAT.

LISTENING TO TONE IN MUSIC

❋ let's "see" what we hear

DARK . . . . **LOW** ♪♪♪. . . . .

Can you imagine a scene that is . . . . . .
{ frightening? heavy? gloomy? sinister? }

e.g. "DAGGER DANCE" by Herbert.

LIGHT . . . . — **HIGH**

What are you imagining? something . . . .
{ airy? fresh? sparkling? fragile? }

e.g. "BALLET OF THE UNHATCHED CHICKS" by Moussorgsky.

GRADED . . . . **LOW** ↗ **HIGH** or vice versa

What is happening? Is it . . . .
{ exciting? spectacular? stirring? }

e.g. "IN THE HALL OF THE MOUNT-AIN KING" by Grieg.

CONTRASTING . . . . — **LOW** ↗ **HIGH** ↘

What do you see in your "mind's eye"? Is it . . . .
{ lively? busy? bright? dynamic? }

e.g. "LEAP FROG" by Bizet.

SIMILAR . . . . **ALL HIGH** OR **ALL LOW** OR **ALL MIDDLE-ISH**

What can you see in your imagination? Is it . . . .
{ ordinary? non-descript? pleasant? boring? }

e.g. "WALKING SONG" by Thomson.

Make a tape of "tonal" music.

N.B. See TEXTURE, p. 48, re source of suggested music pieces.

CREATING TONE IN SOUND · WRITING ABOUT TONE

❋ select your instruments

Use the "SET-UP SITUATIONS" in Activity 8, p.16 and add **SOUND EFFECTS.**
Guide the students into selecting SUITABLE instruments.

Softness makes light sounds lighter.

Loudness makes dark sounds darker.

e.g. **DARK** –
heavy
threatening
spooky

BASS DRUM ROLL with 2 beaters

LIGHT TO **DARK** –
exciting
stirring

start with TRIANGLE GRADED INTO BASS DRUM
CRESCENDO
soft → loud

LIGHT –
delicate
light-hearted

small
triangle

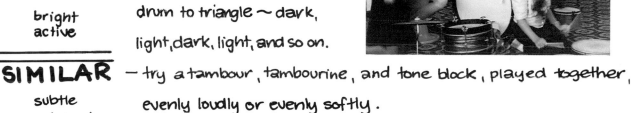

CONTRASTING – jump from bass
bright
active
drum to triangle ~ dark,
light, dark, light, and so on.

SIMILAR – try a tambour, tambourine, and tone block, played together,
subtle
subdued
evenly loudly or evenly softly.

If not using instruments, try tins, saucepans, spoons, knitting needles, and so on.

❋ writing about tone

Write a **story** involving situations with dark and/or light, e.g. about
living in the Land of the Midnight Sun, in a sea cave, or in a rabbit warren. If it was
turned into a **play**, how would the **lighting effects** go?

Write **poems** about dark, light, etc. Start the ball rolling …

"The dark is . . . . [a time for sleeping],

The light is . . . . [a time for fun],

But darkness fading into light

Is . . . . [just because the day's begun]."

MAKING USE OF TECHNOLOGY   computer

✳ let's consolidate on the computer

DEVELOP A SUBJECT ~

Using drawings collected from the environment, e.g. of trees, transfer the tones onto the screen ... move them around ... experiment ... make patterns with REPETITION ... put dark background around light shapes ... try graded tones from light to dark, using different methods ~ dots, crosses, etc. ~ try some negative shapes, as in the sample at right, below. [See also, SHAPE, Activities 36 - 39, pp. 54 - 56.] A simple method of producing negative shapes is to fill in a large shape, then use the "eraser" to draw the positive shape. The negative shapes will remain. In the sample below, at right, these shapes have then been outlined. Note how the positive shape extends beyond the shaded area.

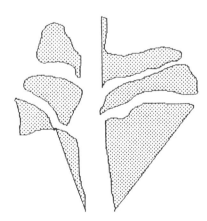

The tree

Penisula School, Mt. Eliza, Victoria.

DISPLAY THE PRINT-OUTS. LET OTHER CLASSES SEE PARTS OF THEIR SCHOOL ENVIRONMENT TRANSLATED INTO COMPUTER GRAPHICS.

COLLECTION AND DISPLAY OF WORDS

✳ This is a 'BIG' MOMENT ~ a tally of the vocabulary that has been collected so far.

LET'S CHECK AND ORGANISE A READY- REFERENCE BANK FOR THE FUTURE

Collect all the words and good phrases USED, HEARD or SEEN and add any more you wish from

- your collected list
- a dictionary
- the Art program
- a thesaurus

OR  memory

 BEST IDEA ...If you haven't already done so, put these words onto WORD CARDS for future resources, displays, and so on.

SEE NEXT PAGE.

 DISPLAY ALL THE WORDS AND GOOD PHRASES FOR THE CLASS TO SEE.

COLLECTION AND DISPLAY OF WORDS

some words related to tone...

PHYSICAL TYPES

light
dark
medium
graded
variegated
similar
contrasting

LIGHT

airy
pure
glary
sparkling
blazing
shimmering
radiant
lustrous
vivid
resplendent
luminous
scintillating
incandescent
fresh
free
light-hearted
happy
delicate
fragile

DARK

heavy
dreary
foreboding
dull
threatening
sombre
stifling
intimidating
claustrophobic
frightening
gloomy
sinister
secure
nocturnal
vespertine
spooky
scary
sad

VARIEGATED TONES

motley
speckled
patchy
uneven
pebbly
peppery
stippled
spattered

like...
fading day
camouflage
bushland
tapestry

CONTRASTING TONES

stark
lively
dramatic
demanding
domineering
dominating
bossy
imposing
powerful
exciting
emphatic
startling
aggressive
spectacular
drastic
dynamic
definitive
distinct
brutal
busy
bright
clear

SIMILAR TONES

monotonous
vague
subdued
nebulous
vaporous
relaxing
comfortable
liquid
ordinary
congenial

GRADED TONES

fading
shadowy
gentle
sensitive

Note the scarcity of descriptive words one could expect from Primary level children. Is this because TONE has not achieved the importance of COLOUR in our everyday world? Describing any object by colour is sufficient on most occasions. Apart from the awareness of very dark and very light, most adults are equally insensitive to TONE, and are unaware of it except when called upon to describe a colour, e.g., "It's <u>dark</u> blue." However, the use of SUITABLE tone is essential in the production of visuals ~ from a creative expression to a road sign!

SECTION TWO

Practical experiences

CONSTRUCTIONS IN ALL-
WHITE PAPER OR POLY-
STYRENE DEPEND ON
TONAL DIFFERENCES FOR
THEIR FORM. THEY PRO-
VIDE THE MUCH-NEEDED
PRACTICE IN **SEEING**
TONES, SO THE "LOOKING
AT" IS AS IMPORTANT AS
THE "MAKING OF." SEE
ACTIVITY 26, p. 32.

YEAR 6

● <u>EXPERIENCE IN THE MOST SUITABLE MEDIUM</u> ~ PAINT · CHARCOAL
  · EXPERIMENTAL "PLAY" – paint
  · DIRECTED EXPERIENCE – charcoal
  · APPLIED EXPERIENCE – charcoal

● <u>OTHER MEDIA AND TECHNIQUES</u>: pencil techniques ; drawing from
   life; paper work [collage silhouettes, paper weaving, paper construction];
   some tone study [atmospheric perspective, basic principles of light and
   shade, light and shade on basic forms]

● "DOING YOUR OWN THING" TIME

EXPERIMENTAL "PLAY"   painting

Paint..... tones, tones, tones

Let students experiment with **WHITE** and **BLACK** paint. They will soon discover **GREY**, and that the black is very strong. Give each student only half as much black paint as white. Draw attention to the student who produces a very light grey. How was it made? With only a very small "touch" of black in the white? Or was more and more white added to black? Watch that <u>too</u> much water isn't added to the paint so that the grey is always watery and weak. Use the tone vocabulary — dark, light, medium dark, lightish, etc. This need not be a long session. It could also be done in small groups throughout the week, at a desk set up for the activity. Let the students learn from each other — they can be effective teachers. If the class is experienced, let them experiment further with black and white paint. Try painting on black or grey paper, on aluminium foil, on black plastic...

Even experienced painters can learn new possibilities of the expressiveness of tones when engaged in experimental play.

✳   EXPERIMENTAL "PLAY" IS **NOT** A WASTE OF TIME, PAINT AND PAPER. IT SERVES TO **SAVE** EACH OF THOSE IN THE FUTURE. IT IS THE LEARNING GROUND FOR ESSENTIAL **CONFIDENCE**, AND FOR MANY THINGS THE TEACHER MAY TAKE FOR GRANTED THE STUDENT KNOWS, e.g. What a painting rag is for.

[The rag is for soaking up excess water from the cleaned brush — and for cleaning up little spills.]

a wall chart discussion

EXPERIMENTAL "PLAY"

MAKE A WALL CHART ~   black, white, greys

Cut interesting snippets from the students' experimental work and DISCUSS.

Add descriptive words to chart.

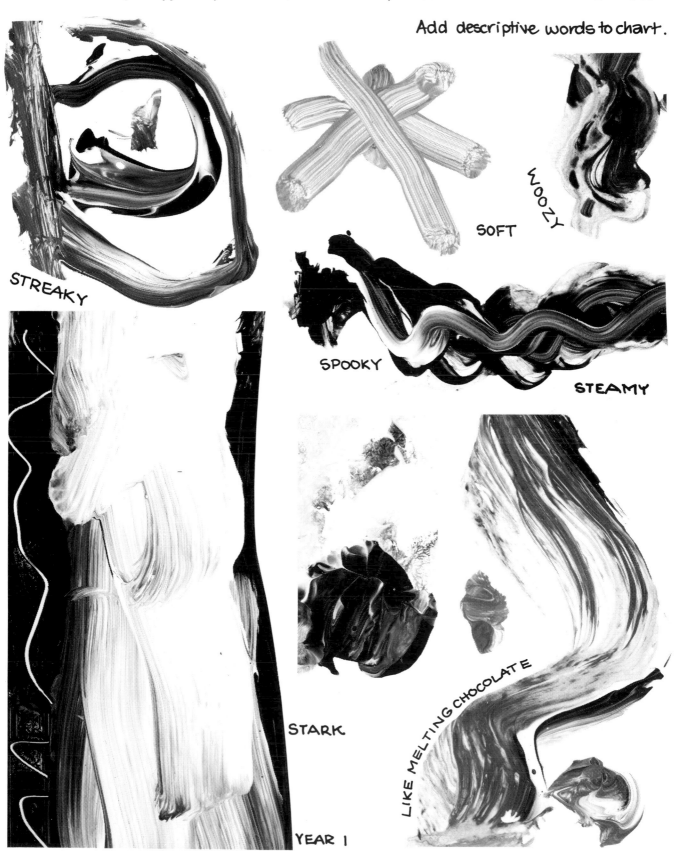

STREAKY

SOFT

WOOZY

SPOOKY

STEAMY

STARK

LIKE MELTING CHOCOLATE

YEAR 1

TONE **25**

DIRECTED EXPERIENCE   charcoal techniques

EXPERIMENT WITH CHARCOAL TECHNIQUES ～

N.B. The quality of charcoal is important. Thin, round, cheap charcoal is scratchy and breaks easily. There is cheap loosely compressed charcoal available in long blocks that will produce beautiful effects. Break each piece in half～ about 3cm lengths. Making your own? Burn green, peeled Pencil Willow stems in a tin. Try other timbers. Experiment on different papers. Newsprint is very good.

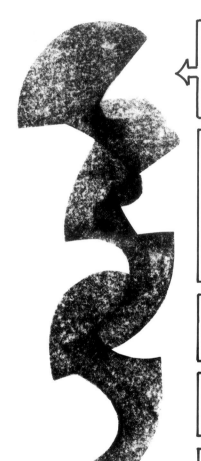

Hold the charcoal on its corner edge and do "**THE SWIVEL**" from side to side, twisting wrist.

PRINT by tapping corner edge ～ move along in little jumps in all directions, including in a circle to make "spokes". Print also with the end, and flat side.

Just **SCRUB**, backwards and forwards ～ heavily or softly

Scrub a little, then **SMUDGE** with fingers, tissue, rag...

ROLL the block charcoal backwards and forwards under the palm of the hand — for fences, rail-way tracks...

Now draw and print just with the charcoal that has come off on the **fingers** or the palm of the **hand**. [Whole drawings can be done this way.]

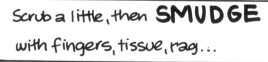

charcoal techniques

DIRECTED EXPERIENCE

Try the **"SWIZZLE"**, rolling the charcoal on its point, between fingers and thumb; or zig-zag left to right, left to right.

Students love **DOTTING** — it's noisy and easy — and spreads like measles.

Cut **GROOVES** in a corner edge with a finger-nail, thin plastic, etc. and just draw lines. Write some words.

COMBINE some techniques in one line

Try **"SHUNTING"** along, pushing the charcoal ahead, back a little, further ahead, back again, and so on.

Scrub over an area with charcoal, then smudge it with a rag or paper, then using an eraser **RUB OUT** lines, i.e. draw with the eraser. Try it without doing the smudging also.

Now... wash hands ~ and faces?! ~ with **SOAP** and water. Charcoal comes out of clothes in the wash ~ no problem at all.

<u>N.B.</u> See photograph on p. 37 for students at work.

APPLIED EXPERIENCE   charcoal

Charcoal work can be "fixed" with commercially prepared fixative ~ otherwise use hair-spray. Two coats should stop any smudging.

Use the techniques in Activity 18 to make a drawing of a particular subject. Plant forms, under-water "gardens" and the bush are good subjects because they are more free than static objects such as houses and machinery.

DISPLAY SOME OF THE WORK.

YEAR 8

EXPERIMENT WITH PENCIL TECHNIQUES

PENCIL TECHNIQUES

Start with 2B or 4B pencils.

The humble pencil remains the easiest, cheapest, non-threatening medium of all, yet its expressive potential is boundless. With practice and high expectations, students can achieve a very high level of technical skill, especially with graded shading. A few minutes practice squeezed into the school day can prove invaluable. Project work will give evidence of improved quality.

EXPERIMENT WITH DIFFERENT PENCILS ON DIFFERENT PAPERS

[harder ← 6H ← 4H ← 2H ← HB → 2B → 4B → 6B → softer]
H means hard, light ← | → B means soft, dark

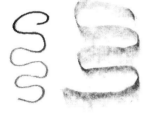

① ON POINT; ON SIDE

② SCRUBBING ~ on point; on side

③ GRADED SHADING ~ start gently, back and forth, pressing more heavily as you go. Go back over it until grading is even.

④ SMUDGING ~ some scrubbing, then rubbing with fingers, rag, etc.

⑤ ERASING ~ draw with eraser through some smudging

⑥ STIPPLING ~ dotting with the point

⑦ HATCHING ~ strokes with the point

⑧ CROSS-HATCHING

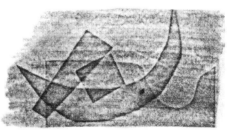

⑨ FROTTAGE ~ rub pencil over paper with flat pieces of paper, etc. underneath – or over rough surface.

⑩ COMBINATIONS of above

TONE **29**

NOW LET'S APPLY THE TECHNIQUES   pencil

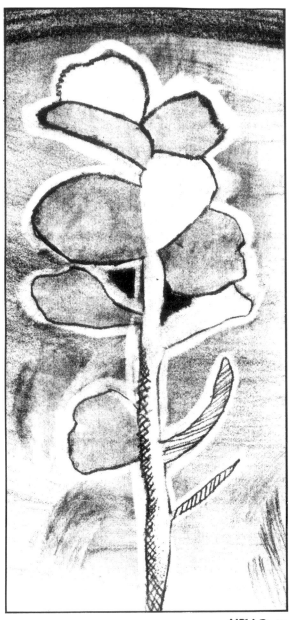

YEAR 7

21 Apply the techniques from Activity 20 to a subject, e.g. something from the collection display or plant forms from the garden, or something from the imagination. Remember to keep tones ~ the darks and lights ~ in mind. List the techniques so none is missed. To make the composition well unified, see Activity 22, below, and the TEACHER'S GUIDE, p. 36 on Unity. Try all these techniques in pastel also. Which ones are suitable for ink?

22 In a composition of many shapes, there is often the problem of hotch-potch. To unify the conglomeration, CONTRAST of TONE can be used between the "centre of interest" area and the background. In tonal study it is called CHIAROSCURO [pro. kiro-<u>sku</u>-ro]. Observe it in Rembrandt's work.

unity through tone

YEAR 6

pencil · charcoal · paint · ink   DRAWING FROM LIFE

Drawing from life is the best learning ground for the "seeing" required for good drawing. No genuine attempts should ever be adversely criticised. Keep looking to the future. Select objects to draw that have strong tones from dark to light. Use a soft pencil, e.g. 4B. Charcoal or black, white and grey pastels are also effective.

YEAR I

Paint from life also, e.g. in MONOCHROME. See COLOUR, p. 38.

◄ A bowl of fruit, jug, bottle and feather duster — a seemingly dull subject. Note the true portrayal of the textures as well as tones. Try some ink — but <u>do</u> wear smocks.

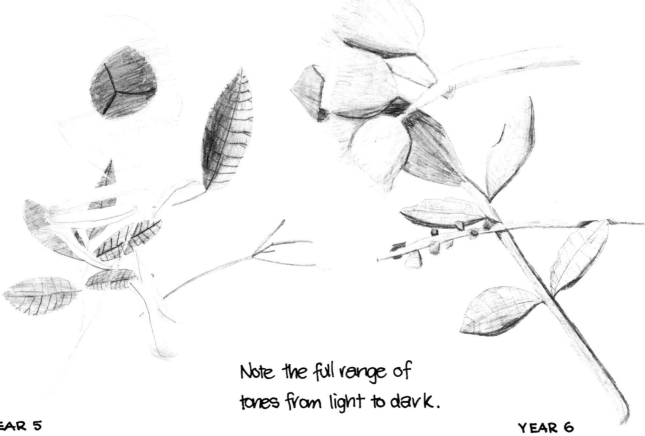

Note the full range of tones from light to dark.

YEAR 5   **YEAR 6**

WORKING WITH PAPER

24 collage silhouettes

YEAR 5

<u>CONTRAST OF DARK AND LIGHT TONES</u>

Students can draw profiles of classmates, cut them out and glue them onto a contrasting background ~ in black SILHOUETTE on white, or vice versa.

25 paper weaving

YEAR 3

Weave strips of white, black and grey [brown paper works quite well also]. Observe the <u>DARK</u>, <u>LIGHT</u> AND <u>MEDIUM</u> TONAL PATTERN. Note how the contrasting tones "jump".

26 paper construction ~ cut, fold, twist...

Make a paper sculpture or structure. Just crumpled paper? Take time to observe the soft, GRADED TONES.

See also, p. 23.

YEAR 5   YEAR 8

creating depth   ATMOSPHERIC PERSPECTIVE

Try a soft pencil or charcoal for the following:

YEAR 6

See also, SHAPE, Activity 35, page 54

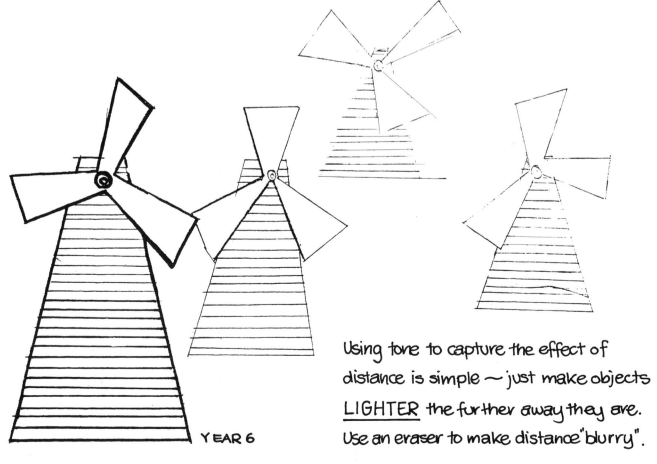

YEAR 6

Using tone to capture the effect of distance is simple ~ just make objects LIGHTER the further away they are. Use an eraser to make distance "blurry".

BASIC PRINCIPLES OF LIGHT AND SHADE

- The <u>CLOSER</u> to the source of light, the <u>LIGHTER</u> the surface of the object.

- The more <u>DIRECT</u> the rays hit the surface, the <u>LIGHTER</u> that surface ~ easily observed on the cube more subtly graded on the curved surfaces.

- Light rays do not travel around corners, but they do <u>REFLECT</u>, bouncing back off other surfaces around the object. Study the photographs below. Note how light reflects back off white surfaces, but not the black. It is worth setting up objects as below, in a dark place, with ONE source of light only.

creating 3D effect   LIGHT AND SHADE ON BASIC FORMS

Try a soft pencil for the following.

The use of shading can make shapes appear 3 dimensional — solid or hollow. If no model is available to observe in suitable lighting, the following formulae for tonal patterns are "fool-proof". In real life, the tones would be more varied because of multiple light sources and near-by reflective surfaces.

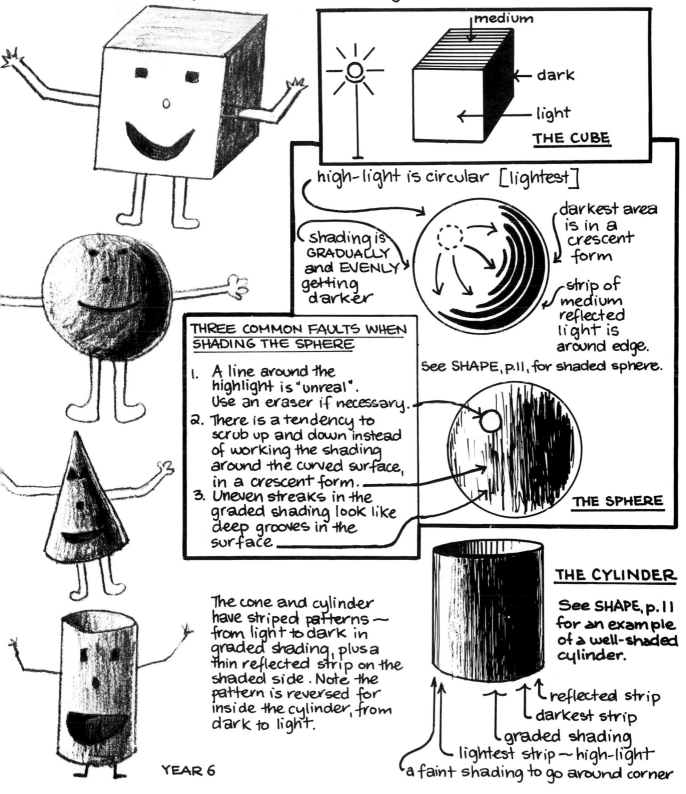

medium

dark

light

THE CUBE

high-light is circular [lightest]

shading is GRADUALLY and EVENLY getting darker

darkest area is in a crescent form

strip of medium reflected light is around edge.

See SHAPE, p.11, for shaded sphere.

THREE COMMON FAULTS WHEN SHADING THE SPHERE

1. A line around the highlight is "unreal". Use an eraser if necessary.
2. There is a tendency to scrub up and down instead of working the shading around the curved surface, in a crescent form.
3. Uneven streaks in the graded shading look like deep grooves in the surface

THE SPHERE

The cone and cylinder have striped patterns — from light to dark in graded shading, plus a thin reflected strip on the shaded side. Note the pattern is reversed for inside the cylinder, from dark to light.

THE CYLINDER

See SHAPE, p.11 for an example of a well-shaded cylinder.

reflected strip
darkest strip
graded shading
lightest strip ~ high-light
a faint shading to go around corner

YEAR 6

TONE **35**

AND . . .

"DOING YOUR OWN thing" TIME

Give . . . , as many opportunities as possible for the students to select their **own subjects**, their **own media and techniques** and their **own time limits**. Try to provide some organized arrangement where they can work on something started on a previous occasion. If they have particular interests, you may be able to have relevant books recommended by the Librarian, handy for them.

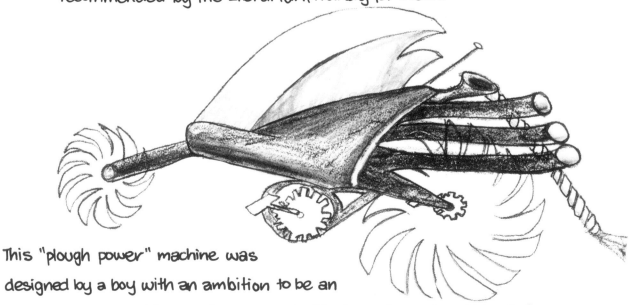

This "plough power" machine was designed by a boy with an ambition to be an inventor. Note how his use of tone has clarified the dimension of depth for us.

SECTION THREE

Evaluation

OBSERVE the student at work ~ to assess confidence, self-reliance, application of knowledge, manipulative skills, work habits, and so on.

"ARE YOU HAPPY WITH WHAT YOU HAVE DONE, ALLISON?"

DOES THE STUDENT NEED HELP?

TALK to the student ~ establish the intentions and compare with results. Was the selection of medium, technique and types of tones suitable for the subject? Were the intentions directed toward the REALISTIC RECORD, the EXPERIMENTAL, INTELLECTUAL, IMAGINATIVE, DECORATIVE, AESTHETIC, or as PERSONAL EXPRESSION ~ or as PRACTICE? See pp. 38-44.

"WHAT IS IT ABOUT, JEFF?" "WHY DID YOU USE THOSE TONES, GWEN?"

LOOK at the student's work in relation to all experiences covered so far. Has knowledge been applied? TAKE THE WORK HOME. GIVE IT A GOOD "SEEING" ~ READ IT AS IF IT WAS WRITTEN TO YOU, PERSONALLY. Every mark a student makes means something, so don't miss it.

COMPARE the student's work with previous work. Is he or she trying <u>new</u> things or simply repeating "successful" formulae?

See <u>EVALUATION</u> section in <u>TEACHER'S GUIDE</u>, pp. 57-59.

What to look for—

See TEACHER'S GUIDE, pp. 50-55.

DON'T FORGET TO CONSIDER THE TEMPERAMENTS ~ only <u>some</u> students are like us.

REALISTIC RECORD

Jose YEAR 7

Tim YEAR 1

Both these drawings are of considerable merit. In each case, the focus is on depicting the tones of the subject. At top, the tones are used to show the three-dimensional form of the hollow gumnut. At left, a sprouting potato shouts the child's awareness of its tones. See Activity 23, p. 31.

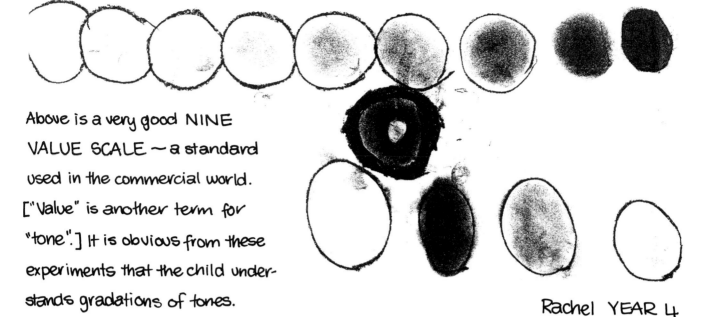

Above is a very good NINE VALUE SCALE ~ a standard used in the commercial world. ["Value" is another term for "tone".] It is obvious from these experiments that the child understands gradations of tones.

Rachel YEAR 4

Pat YEAR 1

Don't underestimate the value of experimenting. While studying students' exploratory samples, you can often see their minds at work. Help them study these samples themselves by pointing out what they have achieved, if only by accident. Note how, for instance, in the painted circles above, the darkest ones stand out strongly because of their CONTRAST with the light background. Also, the dark ones look a little closer to us.

INTELLECTUAL

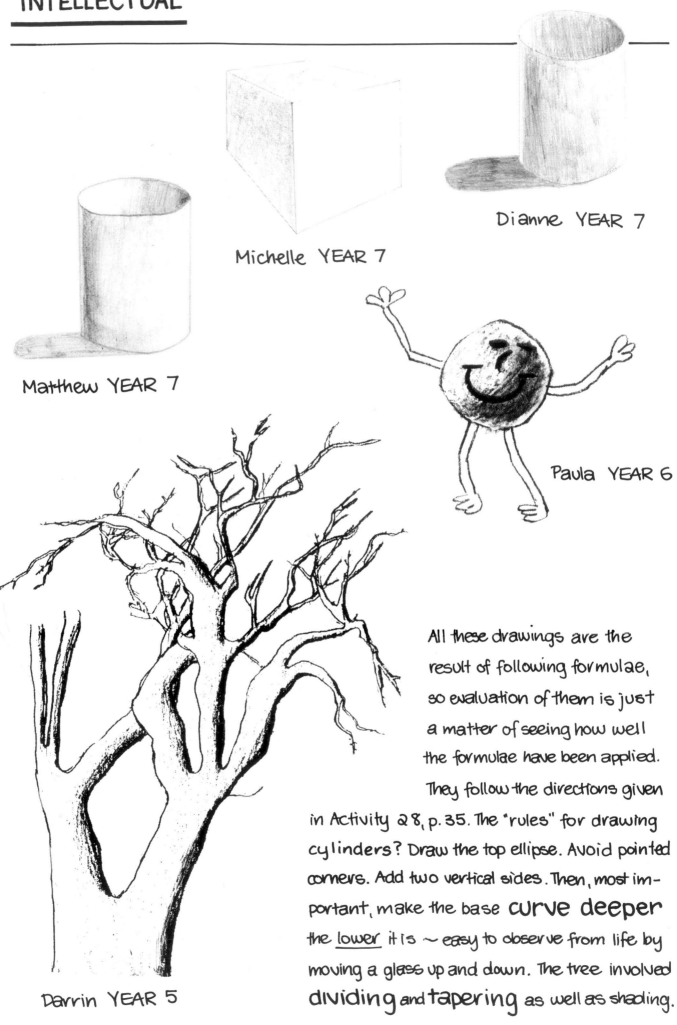

Dianne YEAR 7

Michelle YEAR 7

Matthew YEAR 7

Paula YEAR 6

All these drawings are the result of following formulae, so evaluation of them is just a matter of seeing how well the formulae have been applied.

They follow the directions given in Activity 28, p. 35. The "rules" for drawing cylinders? Draw the top ellipse. Avoid pointed corners. Add two vertical sides. Then, most important, make the base **curve deeper** the <u>lower</u> it is ~ easy to observe from life by moving a glass up and down. The tree involved **dividing** and **tapering** as well as shading.

Darrin YEAR 5

Melinda YEAR 4

Britt YEAR 3

The amazing work above, a collage made from shapes cut from adhesive paper, is a very sophisticated composition depicting the famous Melbourne Cup horse race. Note the flow of overlapping horses balanced by the results board, all linked up by the rail and finishing post. Interest has been added by way of a fallen jockey and perverse white horse. Drama has been created by CONTRAST of tone. This is quite an achievement for a Year 4 child! On left, is a beautifully provocative atmosphere, created almost entirely with tone ~ a few scratchy lines suggest a beaky, witch-like creature.

DECORATIVE

Jodi YEAR 6

This work started out as a practice piece in a Daily Drawing Book [sheets of 16 X 20 cm computer paper stapled together, kept under the desk for any spare moments in the classroom]. The aim was to use graded tones, light to a dark centre, for a hole down into the earth, and graded tones, dark to a light centre, for a tunnel with light at the end. However, as the work progressed, the alternate arrangement became decorative. The whole pattern was completed by a **COUNTER-CHANGE** treatment. [see also, LINE, Activity 30, p. 59.] Credit goes to the initiative shown to turn a practice piece to aesthetic purpose, contributing quite an interesting idea to our world of design.

Bronwyn YEAR 4

In the adhesive paper collage, above, the pieces are meticulously placed. [See SHAPE, Activities 36, 37, p. 54.] The whole is tightly controlled. The charcoal work, below left, however, is free with moving, indefinite edges. The pencil piece, below right, has enough control to keep components centralized and safe, with some energy lines being "allowed" to escape, but with floating shapes organized in a tidy row. Certain media and techniques suit some students' temperaments. Some do not. When evaluating, do keep this in mind. See TEACHER'S GUIDE, pp. 50-55. Which media and techniques on this page suit which temperaments?

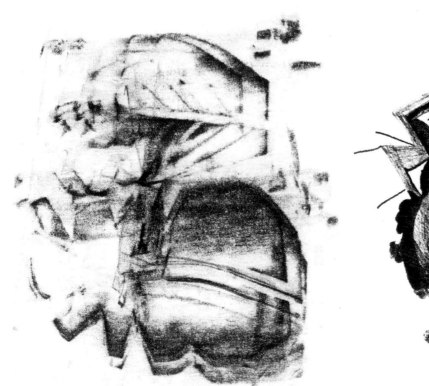

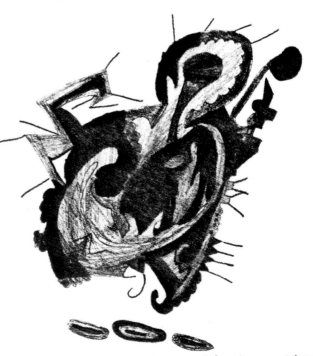

Monique YEAR 6

Samantha YEAR 5

PERSONAL EXPRESSION

In this drawing, "I get mad when Mum tells me to turn T.V. off," note how well the dark areas express the "dark" emotions of both parties. Remember, when evaluating works of personal expression, you are a "listener", and how children "talk" to you is how they _need_ to, in their own way. So evaluation is all about how well their feelings have been expressed ~ in this case, through tone. Had the drawing at right been done in normal, every-day tones, the drama of the situation would have been lost ~ this situation is "beyond mundane realities"!

Anthony YEAR 7

PRACTICE

This drawing was discovered in a Daily Drawing Book, following Activities 20 and 21, pp. 29, 30. The shape just grew according to whim, but its value is far from being mindless. It has afforded the student the opportunity to practise making visual, something that previously had no form. By applying light and shade to it, he has been able to communicate its three-dimensional attributes. He has proven also, to himself, that he can cause to materialise, completely original concepts, an ability that will be useful all his life.

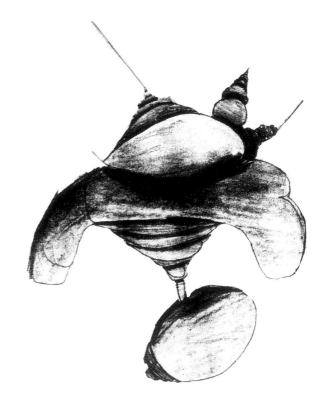

Jason YEAR 6

Notes on Displays

IN THE CLASSROOM —

- Display <u>EVERY</u> student's <u>work</u> at some time.
- <u>CHANGE IT</u> often — seek assistance from a parent, aide, or the students themselves.
- <u>MOUNT</u> the work — attach to a backing sheet.
- <u>LABEL</u> the work — make it work for you!

IN THE SCHOOL OR COMMUNITY —

The local Library usually welcomes displays. Mount the work as "professionally" as possible. It is worth the trouble. Label the pieces so the public knows what the students are about. Themes are popular.

Rhythms of the Land, Sea and Sky — Black Chromacryl on old sheets pinned together — by children of School of the Air, at Charleville, Queensland. [A Queensland Arts Council Activity, 1986]

Texture

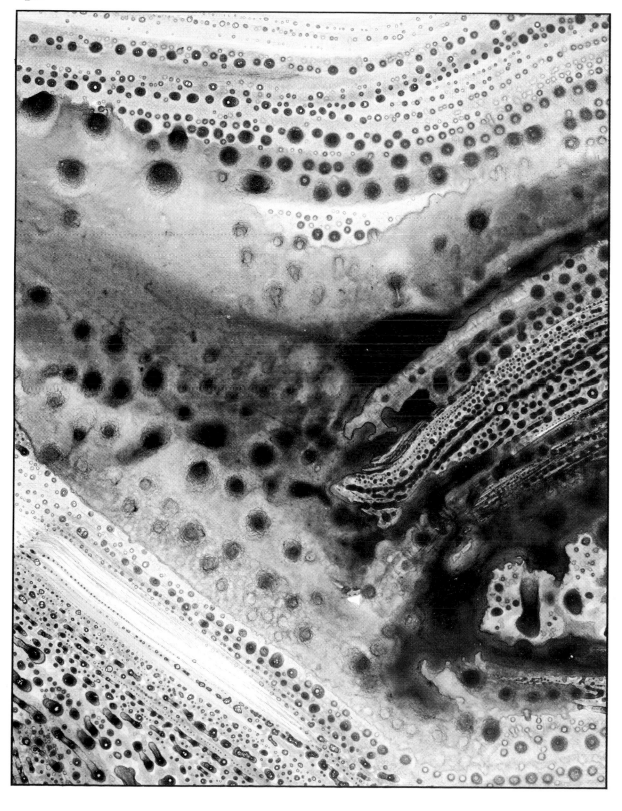

Texture

I sat as a giant in the puddle of the sea and reached out with both my hands to touch the textures of the land. I ran my finger along the smooth, warm tar of the roadways, and pressed my palms into the soft damp foliage of inland forests ~ I scraped my closed fist across the rugged ridges of rocky cliff faces, then soothed them in the squelch of cool mud along the river banks. I ran them over the bumps and baubles of buildings and bridges until they could have crackled beneath my hands like biscuit crumbs. Then I rested them in the sea and closed my eyes to remember the feel of the surfaces of the land.

Contents

TEXTURE is . . . the feel of a substance when touched, or how it appears it would feel when touched — rough, smooth, fluffy, gritty, crumbly, prickly, etc.

SUGGESTED WORK PLAN FOR A BLOCK UNIT OF 5 WEEKS ON TEXTURE

Mix 'n' match your own activities if not following the plan below. Be flexible!

This plan contains every Activity, so reduce according to your timetable. See N.B. below.

WEEK ONE

AWARENESS: Feeling Texture — ACTIVITY 1...pp.8,9. Vocabulary brainstorming
Seeing Texture — ACTIVITY 2...p.10. Seeing and touching safari
PRACTICAL: Experimental "play" — ACTIVITY 18...pp.30,31. Collage

WEEK TWO

AWARENESS: Seeing Texture — ACTIVITY 8...p.18. Texture display
ACTIVITY 9·25...p.19·36. Drawing from life · Pencil
Integration — ACTIVITY 14...p.24. Photocopying
PRACTICAL: Directed experience — ACTIVITY 19...p.32. Painting

WEEK THREE

AWARENESS: Seeing Texture — ACTIVITY 3...pp.11,12. Audio-Visuals. Display
ACTIVITY 5...p.15. Untimetabled discussion
Integration — ACTIVITY 15...p.25. Computer Graphics
PRACTICAL: Applied experience — ACTIVITY 20...p.33. Painting ⎫
Other media — ACTIVITY 27...p.37. Painting ⎬ 4 groups
ACTIVITY 30...p.39. Painting ⎪
ACTIVITY 31...p.39. Painting ⎭

WEEK FOUR

AWARENESS: Seeing Texture — ACTIVITY 4...pp.13,14. Appreciation. [student's Book]
ACTIVITY 6...p.16. Appreciation; Houses
ACTIVITY 7...p.17. Appreciation; Ethnic objects
Integration — ACTIVITY 13...p.23. Writing. Select one Activity
ACTIVITY 16...p.26. Munch and Talk. Writing
PRACTICAL: Other media — ACTIVITY 21·26·28·29...pp.34·37·38·38
Combine collage, frottage, construction, and modelling in one group project.

WEEK FIVE

AWARENESS: Integration — ACTIVITY 10...p.20. Miming. Video shoot
ACTIVITY 11...p.21. Listening to texture
ACTIVITY 12...p.22. Texture with instruments
Language of Texture — ACTIVITY 17...pp.27·28. Word display
PRACTICAL: Other media — ACTIVITY 22-24...p.35. Collage; Weaving [3 groups]
OR ACTIVITY 32...p.40. "Doing your own thing" time

N.B. Remember that **AWARENESS EXPERIENCES** are to work hand in hand with

PRACTICAL EXPERIENCES so that students have a source for ideas. See N.B. LINE p.5.

Materials

FOR 30 STUDENTS ~ FOR **TEXTURE** UNIT

THE BASIC KIT — double if possible

CHROMACRYL PAINT — all five colours*... pp. 32·33·34·37·39

WOOL, STRING, etc. — 1 kg thrums .... pp. 30·31·35

CHARCOAL — 3 boxes, block, compressed... pp. 19·37

CLAY — ½ block — 13 kg terra cotta... p. 38

GLUE — [powdered] → 1 litre... pp. 30·31·34·35

NATURAL HESSIAN — 7m... pp. 35·38

    Also, if possible ~ ALUMINIUM FOIL — 2 rolls... pp. 32·34

        STEEL WOOL — 10 pads... p. 34

THE BARE BONES KIT

CHROMACRYL PAINT — all five colours*... pp. 32·33·34·37·39

    Also, if possible —   WOOL, STRING, etc.... pp. 30·31·35

                  HESSIAN — 1–7m... pp. 35·38

                  ALUMINIUM FOIL — 2 rolls... pp. 32·34

                  STEEL WOOL — 5 pads... p. 34

                  CLAY — ½ block... p. 38

    MAKE YOUR OWN ~ FLOUR and WATER GLUE... pp. 30·31·34·35

                     CHARCOAL from burnt wood... pp. 19·37

THE *running on* ... THIN AIR KIT

CHROMACRYL PAINT — RED, YELLOW, BLUE*... pp. 32·33·34·37·39

SCAVENGE, SAVE, AND MAKE YOUR OWN, AS FOR ABOVE KITS.

<u>N.B.</u> Teachers with expertise in weaving may require specific materials.

<u>FOR ALL KITS</u> : ⊙ Collection of textured objects ~ pine cones, sponges, sand paper, cotton balls, etc. for discussion and displays.

                  ⊙ Collection of scraps and small, flat, textured objects suitable to glue onto paper/cardboard as collage.

* Commercial names : Cool Yellow, Warm Red, Warm Blue, Black, White.

SECTION ONE

Awareness experiences

AIMS:
- to awaken an interest in texture **for its own sake**
- to develop a **vocabulary** about texture at all levels of awareness ~ physical to abstract

- FEELING TEXTURE
- SEEING TEXTURE
- INTEGRATED EXPERIENCES WITH TEXTURE
- LANGUAGE OF TEXTURE

RESOURCES

RESOURCES: Make a permanent collection of textural objects with as wide a variety as possible. Once used for Activity 1, it can form the basis for displays, be used for drawing from life, for reference, and so on.

... hessian, prickly seed pods, crinkled vegetables, fur, fluff.

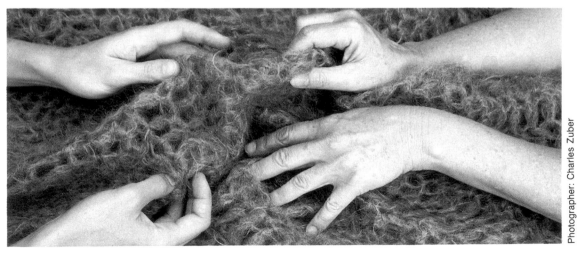

Photographer: Charles Zuber

Textures are most keenly experienced through the sense of touch. Let the expression, "having the world at our fingertips" take on a new meaning for this Activity. It can open up new worlds.

VOCABULARY BRAINSTORMING

THE TALKING TEXTURES SESSION!

STUDENTS CAN SIT IN A CIRCLE. PASS OBJECTS AROUND.

BRAINSTORM!

ENSURE THE STUDENTS ARE
AWARE OF THE TEXTURES.
BRAINSTORM FOR WORDS.
SHARE EXPERIENCES.

"...smooth · crinkly · rubbery ·
spiky · crumbly · frizzy ·
like marshmallows ... "
See pp. 27, 28.

COLLECT THE WORDS

THE STUDENTS USE TO
DESCRIBE THE TEXTURES
OF THE OBJECTS. PUT
THEM ONTO WORD CARDS
FOR FUTURE RESOURCES.

THE SEEING AND TOUCHING SAFARI

AIMS:
- to help the students learn to **SEE**, i.e. to see **more** than the mere physical presence of objects
- to develop further a **VOCABULARY** about texture on all levels of awareness ~ physical to abstract

Set off into the schoolyard, after issuing a few "orders of the day" with respect to taking care when touching things. "Vandals" can be promptly dispensed with ~ it won't stifle their artistic careers. Explore surfaces with eyes and hands. [Take a towel for grubby hands.] **COLLECT WORDS USED.**

"The clouds look soft like dreaming."

"It's scratchy here"   "...slimy and yuk"

"The leaves are smooth"   "I like my furry tummy best"

Have the **camera** ready [black and white will do]. BUILD UP RESOURCES.

DON'T HOLD BACK THE "BIG WORDS". IF STUDENTS CAN SEE AND FEEL A "SLITHERY" TEXTURE, THEY MOST LIKELY CAN UNDER-STAND AND USE IT IN THEIR DRAWINGS.

MAKING THE MOST OF MEDIA

AUDIO-VISUAL RESOURCES:

Lay a card with shapes cut out of it on top of the overhead projector. Fill each shape with some material, e.g. teased cotton wool, sand, hundreds and thousands, cut hair in mass ~ to create different textures on the screen. Shapes could represent animals, e.g. dogs. Build up language.

Investigate sources of videos, films, strips, etc. about COLOUR, and/or make some yourself. Ask school and community Libraries, Education Centres, Film Centres, and so on.

Check the school television and radio broadcasts for Art programs. Timetables are usually available at the beginning of each year. Try to build up the school's resources as well as your own.

WATCH AND DISCUSS.

STATIC RESOURCES:

See next page.

LOOK AND DISCUSS.

DISPLAY in the classroom, or elsewhere in the school ~

- photographs you, or others, have taken
- pictures from magazines
- newspaper photographs
- posters
- record covers, book covers, and so on.

You may have space for only **ONE** photograph in your classroom ~ fine! It will have unrivalled status of importance ~ but do change it often.

MEDIA

classroom display

Collect photographs on a theme. **DISCUSS** display at opportune moments.

TEXTURES OF OUR COUNTRY

Rough, cracked texture of the Cork Tree.

Smooth and crinkled skins of road-side melons.

Photograph: Clive Pope, Queensland

Crumbly, grooved limestone shores of Western Australia.

Splintery, stringy trees from King's Canyon in the Northern Territory.

APPRECIATION IN THE WORLD OF ART

DISCUSS the Art Works below in conjunction with the Student's Book, pp. 4, 9, 10 and 16.

How would these surfaces feel to touch? ... like flaky paper? rough granite? silk? goose bumps?

The sculptured facade of this French Cathedral is not only textural. It also teaches stories of the Bible.

120 x 90 cm

Courtesy of the artist

"DAWN" by Jeanne MACASKILL [b. 1931 N.Z.] Mixed media on board. 1985. This artist often uses haberdashery such as buttons for textural effects.

Courtesy of Jon Tupou, Queensland

Tapa cloth from Tonga, with traditional symbols. Note the textural effect of the beaten bark.

Show the students some work by Van Gogh. Note the textures.

APPRECIATION IN THE WORLD OF ART

153 x 200 x 160 cm Purchased 1981

Courtesy of the National Gallery of Victoria

Courtesy of Kate Fox, Queensland

" <u>DIALOGUE</u>" by Ewa PACHUKA [b. 1936 POLAND] Crocheted sisal, manila and coir over wire armature and cardboard cylinder. 1973–78.

Maori tiki, wood and shell inlay.

String, wire, cardboard, wood, shell, cement, bark . . . these are familiar materials. Discuss how artists have crocheted, carved, moulded, glued and beaten them into beautiful forms.

Photograph: John Thorpe, Tasmania

Barong dance, Bali, with highly textured costumes.

150 x 50 x 30 cm

Collection of Tim Foley, Queensland

"<u>SEAL</u>" by Kath SHILLAM [b. 1916 ENG.] Ciment fondu. Note the waxy, "moist" texture.

APPRECIATION IN THE STUDENT'S OWN WORLD

This is an informal, untimetabled activity that can occur all the year round...whenever textures present themselves.

Some can take it rough !

Some are for cuddling . . .
some are for licking off fingers.

As dedicated artists say, "Art is a way of life."
Don't wait for Art lessons to keep students aware of texture. Discuss it whenever opportune.

Some are in the next paddock where the other team hits the cricket ball . . . .   and some you don't dare touch!

APPRECIATION IN THE STUDENT'S OWN WORLD

What are the textures of your <u>house</u>?

Ask students to investigate the textures of the building materials of their own houses. They could help make a classroom **chart** like this one.

CAN YOU PICK THE...

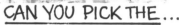

- scaly Welsh shingled house?
- crumbly French artist's quarters?
- fibrous Fijian bure?
- splintery Swiss log cabin?
- velvety thatched English cottage?
- gritty Scottish castle?

APPRECIATION OF ETHNIC OBJECTS AT HOME

Courtesy of Heather Joseph, Queensland

These Lebanese dolls show the textures of the traditional dress.

A quick walk around the home often reveals articles typical of particular cultures ~ a ceramic swagman, a stars-and-stripes plastic hat, a sequined Indian elephant, a smooth Maori tiki, a Chinese silk wall-hanging. If the students are unable to bring any of these to school, set up a "home search assignment". Ask the students to explore their homes. Parents or older brothers or sisters might help in the search. Discuss these at school the next day. Perhaps put them on display. Find articles yourself to use in the classroom discussion. Does anyone know why the Indonesian ekat is streaky? What are mats often made of that makes them coarse? Which object from home has the nicest texture to touch?

Someone might own a streaky Indonesian ekat cloth

Keep an eye open for articles from other countries and cultures that have strong textural quality. Give your-self a purpose in visiting flea markets and elderly aunts!

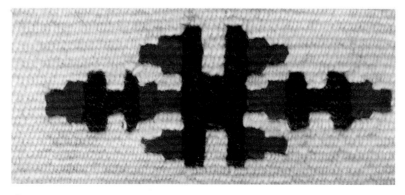

Note how the design fits the coarse texture of this mat from Czechoslavakia [detail]

MAKING A TEXTURE DISPLAY

TEXTURES ON CENTRE STAGE

NATURAL OR MAN-MADE ~ cloth, corrugated cardboard, crinkled silver paper ~ leaves, rocks, bark ...

ON A TABLE, BENCH, SHELF OR DISPLAY BOARD

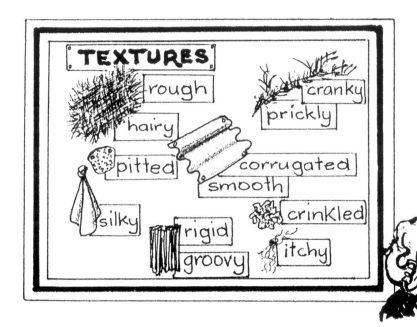

Once the display is in place, simply draw attention to it, **discuss** it briefly now and then, and use it for reference. Older students can set it up completely by themselves.

Visit any artist's studio ~ you are bound to see a "collection" around the walls!

No space in the classroom?

Try . . . . . .
- A "texture a day" ~ each student or group can bring along samples of man-made or natural textured objects to display to the rest of the class, perhaps with a short description or suggestions of words to be added to the classroom list.
- The Library is usually available for displays.
- Flat objects come out well on the **photocopier.** Copies may be kept and objects returned. These copies could be made into books for children to peruse.

RECORDING TEXTURES FROM LIFE

See TEACHER'S GUIDE, pp. 22-27.

The easiest and most valuable lesson of all!

Don't forget the **camera** ~ black and white film will do. Build up your resources.

Collect most of the textures direct. Place paper on the textured surface, [feel it first with the fingers], then rub it over with pencil or charcoal. This technique is called **FROTTAGE** [pro. frot-ahzh]. See LINE, Activity 29, p. 55, and SHAPE, Activity 44, p. 61. Collect textures in the schoolyard and in the classroom. Collect some from home. Discover what places **feel** like ~ or appear to feel like. **DRAW** some textures in the normal way. Pencil Techniques in TONE, Activity 20, p. 29, such as stippling, would be useful.

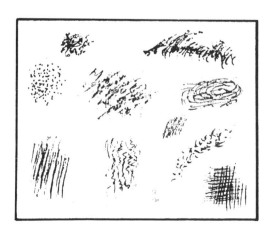

◀ A student's page may look something like this.

Display and discuss, however briefly, all the students' work ~ as a whole. Choose a heading for the display . . . . .

HOW DOES IT FEEL?

USING TEXTURE IN DRAMA AND MOVEMENT

✳ miming textures

Here's one way to start ～

1. Select a student to think of something that has an easily described texture, and to mime rubbing hands over its surface so that the movement indicates the texture. [like playing charades].

2. Ask the class to guess the texture [not the object]. It might be rough, scratchy, splintery, crinkled, jagged, spiky, stubbly, itchy, turbulent...

3. Now think of things that have this texture... a Fijian bure? [See p.16], an iron bark tree? a porcupine? a plucked chook? a short hair cut?

[If the movement is too hard to define, try another. Ideas come slowly, then snowball.]

Professional dancers, actors and film directors, would all be very much aware of texture in movement. "Mr Silvertongue" would need to move "like silk", in keeping with his "smooth talk". Can you move like "true grit?"

Now try a group miming a large textured surface ～

bumpy, stony, like pebbles; goose-bumps

smooth, wavy, like stroking, like a languid sea

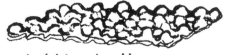

bubble plastic

silk

Here is another opportunity to use the **VIDEO** camera ～ or still camera if no video is available. Try prickles, syrup, popcorn... in body language.

LISTENING TO TEXTURE

❋ let's touch sound

N.B. See TEXTURE, p.48, re source of suggested music pieces.

LISTEN TO SOUNDS. HOW WOULD THEY FEEL IF WE COULD TOUCH THEM?

Imagine the following —

- MAN-MADE SOUNDS . . . . feet shuffling? [furry]

  Imagine the sounds first, . . . an electric fan? [turbulent]
  [perhaps close eyes], . . . screeching brakes? [raspy]
  then put your hands out to
  "touch" the sound. . . . hand clapping? [corrugated]

- NATURAL SOUNDS . . . . wind in the leaves? [shaggy]

  what would
  rustling
  feel like? . . waves in the sand? [gritty]

  . . . running water? [bubbly]

- MUSICAL INSTRUMENTS

  violin — fibrous? elastic? rubbery? like string?

  trumpet — metallic? hard? like silver?

  oboe — smooth? viscous? like syrup?

  maracas — granular? peppery? like a wheat field?

  castanets — rigid? spiky? like a porcupine?

MUSIC

- Listen to the **rough** texture of . . .
  "CIRCUS MUSIC" [from "THE RED PONY"] by Copland, or any
  music with a lot of discord and "rough" instruments.
- Listen to the **smooth** texture of . . .
  "BARCAROLLE" by Offenbach, or any music with smooth
  flowing melody and "liquid" instruments.

Did the composer succeed in expressing the texture of the atmosphere? See
TEACHER'S GUIDE, p.15, the categories of awareness of abstract qualities.

CREATING TEXTURE IN SOUND

✳ select your instruments

[If no instruments are available—improvise.]

Try some of the following ~

- **hard and bumpy** — scrape the old **washing board**, a favourite in bush bands — or a xylophone — or a gyro — or corrugated cardboard

  ...like chewing uncooked rice

  ...like a bumpy road

- **scruffy and prickly** ~ rattle the **lagerphone**, another from the bush band — or maracas ~ or seeds in a tin

  ...like steel-wool

  ...like having the jitters

- **smooth and hard** — try the **recorder** — or trumpet — or just whistle

  ...like liquid silver

  ...like a satin ribbon

- **soft and fluffy**

...like cotton wool

TAPE RECORD THE SOUNDS, PLAY THEM BACK AND DISCUSS THEIR TEXTURES.

Try a drum-roll on a **bass-drum** using soft beaters.

WRITING ABOUT TEXTURE

✳ putting texture into words

a) **poems** ~ Here are some "starters". The students complete ~

The texture of a [comb] is [rough]
The texture of a [rope] is [tough]
The texture of [meringue] is [light]
And [crumbles underneath my bite.] [It doesn't have to rhyme.]

Now, how about some poems that make us want to touch things?

b) **stories** ~ Students could write a report on the textures they encountered as visitors to Earth from another planet as creatures with super-sensitive feeling for touch. Names of objects, of course, would not be known to them . . . "There was this spongy thing to sit on and a hard smooth object to put your elbows on. Outside, wispy, light stuff was drifting around . . ." Can the objects be guessed from their textures?

c) **scripts** ~ Write a simple puppet play with characters dressed in fabrics to suit their personalities.

← smooth black silk

"SLIPPERY SAM
THE SINISTER SPY"

← fluffy cotton wool

― light fluffy material

"FLOSSY FLORENCE
THE FLIPPANT FLORIST"

See COLOUR, Activity 28, p.44.

d) **snippets** ~ Make up names with textures, e.g. Gritty Graham, the Concrete Maker. How does your name sound with a textural twang? Does it suit you? Leathery Laurence? Crinkly Chris?

MAKING USE OF TECHNOLOGY   photocopier

❋ put the photocopier to work

a) Most flat **objects** come out well on the photocopying machine ~ an exciting experience! These photocopies can be displayed easily and the original objects can be returned to their owners. If they are "precious" objects, they are no longer at risk. This can be a small-groups activity, with a teacher-aide, school-secretary, or a parent as machine operator and "artistic director". Otherwise, the teacher could do the photo-copying and show the results to the class.

b) Make some **book-cover paper**, or wrapping paper, by photocopying some flat, textured articles belonging to the students, from the classroom, or from the school-yard ~ a fluffy jumper, satin ribbons, rulers, pencils, pad, fabric, pencil-cases, etc. For extra textural interest, add a textured cloth of contrasting tone over the top, as background. Again, an adult could do the photocopying.

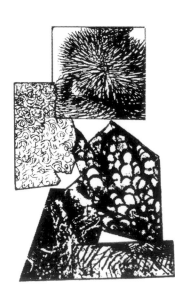

c) Photocopy detailed sections of **illustrations** in books. Ask the Librarian to assist. Find as wide a variety as possible ~ the scaly skin of St. George's dragon; the smooth, shiny leather of Dick Whittington's boots; the fluffy fur of innumerable bears, cats and monkeys. Discuss techniques the artist might have used ~ water-colour and ink, collage, etc. [The Librarian will know the rules of copy-right in relation to study within the school.]

✳ exploring texture on the computer

Excite the brain as well as the eyes . . .

Peninsula School, Mt. Eliza, Victoria.

An easy exploration of texture can develop from a **patch-work** idea. Students can fill shapes with various patterns that suggest textured surfaces. This idea can then be transferred to shapes in a picture.

Textures can be produced by **suitable movement** of the mouse. The raggedness of the tree, at left, was made by "ragged" movement. Ensure students select a subject they can describe with hand movements.

Peninsula School, Mt. Eliza, Victoria.

. . . AND NOW FOR SOMETHING A LITTLE DIFFERENT

✳ have a munch and talk session

1. Collect a variety of foodstuffs — sugar, honey, bread, biscuit, apple, banana, mandarine . . .

2. So that taste is not confused with texture, have a list of textural words somewhere in front of the class —gritty, lumpy, smooth, crunchy, runny, viscous, brittle, crumbly, crisp, soft, squelchy, slimy . . . according to year level.

3. Select several students, blind-fold them, or have them close their eyes and hold their noses. It is more exciting if they don't know what foods they are eating. Give each student a different textured food. Each of them describes the **texture** [not what the food is]. The spectators may be able to guess by the expressions on faces!

If no actual tasting is desired, use foods already known to the students, set out on a table. Use word cards already made up. [See words on p.28.] Ask students to match words with textures they associate with the foods. Or, for a **DULL** session, write words on the blackboard and ask students to think of foods that would match. [No food needed.]

Now, write a _Menu_

- for • a man with no teeth
  - • a frustrated person who wants to "take it out on something" [a teacher on a rainy day?]
  - • for someone who believes that "variety is the spice of life."

COLLECTION AND DISPLAY OF WORDS

✳ This is a `BIG` MOMENT ~ a tally of the vocabulary that has been collected so far.

LET'S CHECK AND ORGANISE A READY-REFERENCE BANK FOR THE FUTURE

Collect all the words and good phrases USED, HEARD or SEEN and add any more you wish from

- your collected list
- a dictionary
- the Art program
- a thesaurus

OR

 **BEST IDEA**...If you haven't already done so, put these words onto WORD CARDS for future resources, displays, and so on.

SEE NEXT PAGE.

Now DISPLAY ALL THE WORDS AND GOOD PHRASES FOR THE CLASS TO SEE.

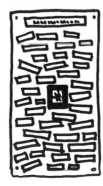

COLLECTION AND DISPLAY OF WORDS

some words related to texture

Make your own list. These are just for reference, to be used if desired.

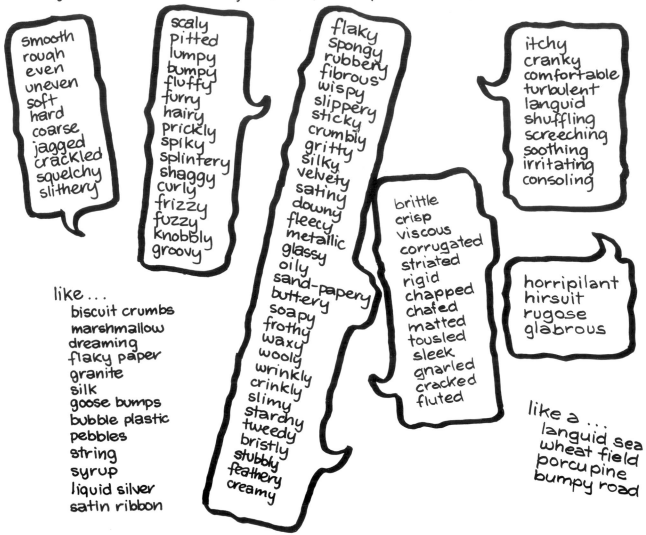

smooth
rough
even
uneven
soft
hard
coarse
jagged
crackled
squelchy
slithery

scaly
pitted
lumpy
bumpy
fluffy
furry
hairy
prickly
spiky
splintery
shaggy
curly
frizzy
fuzzy
knobbly
groovy

flaky
spongy
rubbery
fibrous
wispy
slippery
sticky
crumbly
gritty
silky
velvety
satiny
downy
fleecy
metallic
glassy
oily
sand-papery
buttery
soapy
frothy
waxy
wooly
wrinkly
crinkly
slimy
starchy
tweedy
bristly
stubbly
feathery
creamy

brittle
crisp
viscous
corrugated
striated
rigid
chapped
chafed
matted
tousled
sleek
gnarled
cracked
fluted

itchy
cranky
comfortable
turbulent
languid
shuffling
screeching
soothing
irritating
consoling

horripilant
hirsuit
rugose
glabrous

like ...
biscuit crumbs
marshmallow
dreaming
flaky paper
granite
silk
goose bumps
bubble plastic
pebbles
string
syrup
liquid silver
satin ribbon

like a ...
languid sea
wheat field
porcupine
bumpy road

Of course the students don't have to use or know the particular words above! This is simply a guide to the teacher's own list, irrespective of age or stage of the students. However, remember that a word's degree of difficulty is not dependent on its length. Students know what goose-bumps are, and "horripilant" is not much longer than the name, Elizabeth, and is the same length as "marshmallow". And, of course, the students don't have to write or spell the words ~ they see them on WORD CARDS*, hear the teacher use them, and use them themselves when talking. What a strange world this would be if we could use words, or eat marshmallows, only if we could spell them!

* WORD CARDS are invaluable. Once made they are resources for years.

SECTION TWO
Practical experiences

On the floor is easiest.

"sewing" with sticks ?! See p. 35.

- ● <u>EXPERIENCE IN THE MOST SUITABLE MEDIUM</u> — COLLAGE · PAINT
  - · EXPERIMENTAL "PLAY" - collage
  - · DIRECTED EXPERIENCE - paint
  - · APPLIED EXPERIENCE - paint
- ● <u>OTHER MEDIA AND TECHNIQUES</u>: aluminium foil collage ; textile collage ; wool collage ; weaving ; drawing from life ; frottage ; mixed-media painting ; construction ; modelling ; printing
- ● <u>"DOING YOUR OWN THING" TIME</u>

EXPERIMENTAL "PLAY"   collage

Glue... textures, textures, textures

REQUIREMENTS : paper [preferably from a long roll, or joined so there are no borders to restrict the students] ; glue, in several containers so students can share; a brush for each student; a collection of all manner of textural objects and substances that can be glued onto paper ~ bark, seeds, cellophane, buttons, sand ...

Give students free reign to arrange the textural substances as they wish. Stress they are NOT MAKING A PICTURE ~ but if it happens - so be it ! ~ there's no point in stopping the flow of an idea. Just aim at a **"TREASURE TROVE OF TEXTURES".** Spray with silver paint ?

Experimental "play" is NOT a waste of time, glue and paper! It serves to SAVE each of those in the future. It is the learning ground for essential CONFIDENCE, and for many things the teacher may take for granted the student knows, e.g. glue makes thin paper wrinkle. The activity could be done a hundred times and each time, with different materials and background, could prove a profitable learning experience. Even with ad - vanced and adult classes, it serves as a non-pressure activity which provides freedom for the exploration of textural effects.

So····· guard against a nonchalant attitude that says, in effect, to the students that the only important Art work is a "proper picture"!!

collage

EXPERIMENTAL "PLAY"

If possible, display the frieze with word cards added. At right, we have ~ smooth, shiny, waxy, spongy, flaky, fibrous, viscous, brittle, rigid, scaly, bumpy, splintery, prickly, feathery, itchy, and many more textures to be discovered.

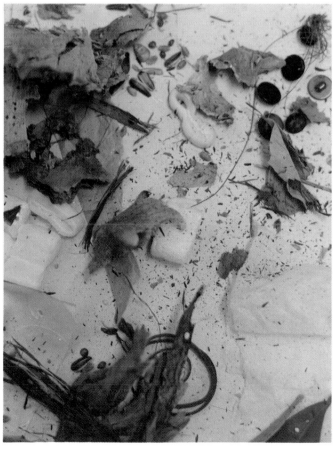

DIRECTED EXPERIENCE

making textures with Paint

[Chromacryl, being a plastic "emulsion", can produce almost any texture you like. If sand or other such substance is added, it will hold like glue. If thin transparency is required, simply add water. It will take to all surfaces, although a "resist" reaction will occur on oily surfaces, which in itself produces interesting textures.]

First, try techniques in LINE, Activity 15, p.45, and COLOUR, Activity 17, pp. 33, 34, such as ~ blob and dribble; dribble and blow; brush rolling; scraping; resist; wet-into-wet; glazing; printing with rag, tissue, fingers; sgraffito; monoprinting; and spattering with a brush.

Now, think in terms of ...

Monoprinting. See p. 39.

• painting on different surfaces — cloth, aluminium foil, plastic sheeting, glossy paper or card, corrugated cardboard, plastic lids, windows ...

• painting with different "tools" — fingers, crumpled paper, wet or dry cloth, stick, spoon, toothbrush, old hairbrush or scrubbing brush, rubber spatula, old broom [on large paper], feather, piece of cord, rubber or sponge roller...

REMEMBER, THIS ACTIVITY IS STILL ABOUT EXPLORING TEXTURES. TEXTURAL EFFECTS ON THE WINDOW PAINTED WITH A BROOM ARE NOT "MESSES". They are cousins to Chartres Cathedral's stained-glass magnificence!

painting   APPLIED EXPERIENCE

<u>NOW LET'S APPLY THE TECHNIQUES</u> discovered in Activity 19.

<u>PAINTING</u>

YEAR 5

Now, let's try applying the various techniques discovered in Activity 19. Give the students the opportunity to develop techniques that appeal to them. So often, painting sessions can turn into "one offs" and students never again receive the opportunity to develop particular skills. The subjects could be from drawings done in previous activities, or from imagination, or from life ... the latter enabling the teacher to discuss the textural qualities first hand. It is quite an interesting exercise for every student to paint the same subject but using a different technique.

YEAR 4

COLLAGE | aluminium foil

YEAR 5

This is an interesting treatment of collage. Pieces of cardboard are cut and glued onto a backing piece of cardboard. A sheet of aluminium foil [from the grocery store] is pressed and glued over the top, easing it into the crevices. It is then painted in black Chromacryl, and when dry, rubbed over with steel-wool to bring out the shapes ~ like a low-relief sculpture. See SHAPE, p.50.

22 textile collage — cloth and string

YEAR 4

Collage is one of the best media for direct experience with textures and can be developed to a high level. It also eliminates problems for students who worry about their drawing, especially in the upper year levels.

23 wool collage

YEAR 4

24 weaving

Hessian weaving requires no special tools. Almost any "line" can be woven through its loose threads — wool, rope, nylon, string, wire, sticks. Show the students how to pull threads right out, or apart to make holes. Young children may need help with rough sticks that catch on the threads. It is simply a matter of threading in and out ~ any direction.

DRAWING FROM LIFE

pencil

. . . TEACHES US TO **SEE** !!!

YEAR 7

◀ This ti-tree swamp, drawn from life while on a school camp, shows great sensitivity to texture. School camps and excursions into new territories are excellent opportunities for drawing from life.

At left, a Year 2 class works quietly at a still-life subject [above], with the teacher joining in.

FROTTAGE· MIXED-MEDIA PAINTING

26 frottage

YEAR 5

Take "rubbings" from surfaces indoors and outdoors. [See Activity 9, p. 19.] Use charcoal or soft pencil on butcher paper or newsprint. To use the technique for picture or pattern making, cut shapes out of textured paper or card. Flat, textured objects such as combs, coins and cloths, can be used also. Note the use of the comb at left. See also TEACHER'S GUIDE, p. 44.

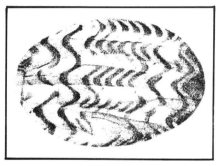

YEAR 8

This "Easter Egg" was taken from the sole of a jogging shoe.

27 mixed-media painting

Encourage and praise the use of texture in all painting ~ it promotes awareness of the aesthetic qualities of paint beyond its mere use for "colouring in an outline." The more practice with textural effects, the sooner the students learn to control paint. Provide students with other materials, e.g. tissues, cellophane, sand... to mix with paint. It acts as glue.

"Monster"

YEAR 2

CONSTRUCTION　　　　　modelling

28 construction

Try to find building
materials with as wide
a variety of textures as
possible ~ blocks of wood,
polystyrene, cardboard,
etc. No gluing or joining
need be done. Rely on
balancing and leaning.
Remember that the focus
is on the use of textural
surfaces. The construc-
tion need not be arch-
itectural. What about
robots or Outer space
furniture?

See also, Activity 6, p. 16.

YEAR 6

This design for a Cultural Centre has large surfaces
to feature texture. Its design and feeling for space
is reminiscent of the early Greek temples, such as the
Parthenon.

29 modelling

YEAR 5

Before making objects, experiment by pressing different textural surfaces onto the
clay ... hessian, soles of jogging shoes, rough stones ... then add texture by adding
"substances" such as sand to the clay. The porcupine above is exuberantly textural !
Note the magazine background in the photograph at left.

30 monoprinting

Using a roller or brush, apply paint onto desk or other smooth surface. [Tape plastic onto desk if not laminated.] Draw into paint with fingers or some sort of scraper. Have a pile of paper close by. Press a sheet down onto the paint and rub [don't bang!] with hands. Lift off.

Notice in the photograph, that the children in the background are working with textural effects in clay. Another group was weaving hessian. If time is short, these different groupings not only save time, but students can see texture in different contexts in the one session. [chromacryl washes off desks easily and leaves no stain.]

31 block printing

Any surface that can be pressed down flat should be suitable for a block. At right, polystyrene gives a sponge-like texture. Cut vegetables such as onions and corn, also provide a wide range of textures.

Polystyrene blocks

YEAR 1

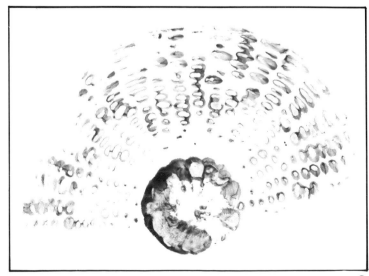

YEAR 3

YEAR 8

AND . . .

"DOING YOUR OWN thing" TIME

Give . . . as many opportunities as possible for the students to select their **own subjects**, their **own media and techniques** and their **own time limits**. This could be on those unpredictable occasions when a student finishes work long before the rest of the class, or when some organized plan goes awry and you are caught unprepared with a whole class to keep profitably employed. Daily Drawing Books are handy for these occasions also.

At right, a child has the opportunity to show his Mum "a thing or two."

SECTION THREE

Evaluation

OBSERVE the student at work ~ to assess confidence, self-reliance, application of knowledge, manipulative skills, work habits, and so on.

"ARE YOU HAPPY WITH WHAT YOU HAVE DONE, ALLISON?"

DOES THE STUDENT NEED HELP?

TALK to the student ~ establish the intentions and compare with results. Was the selection of medium, techniques, and types of textures suitable for the subject? Were the intentions directed toward the REALISTIC RECORD, the EXPERIMENTAL, INTELLECTUAL, IMAGINATIVE, DECORATIVE, AESTHETIC, or as PERSONAL EXPRESSION ~ or as PRACTICE? See pp. 42-47.

"WHAT IS IT ABOUT, JUDY?" "WHY DID YOU USE THOSE TEXTURES, SHELLEY?"

LOOK at the student's work in relation to all experiences covered so far. Has knowledge been applied? TAKE THE WORK HOME. GIVE IT A GOOD "SEEING" ~ READ IT AS IF IT WAS WRITTEN TO YOU, PERSONALLY. Every mark a student makes means something, so don't miss it.

COMPARE the student's work with previous work. Is he or she trying new things or simply repeating "successful" formulae?

See EVALUATION section in TEACHER'S GUIDE, pp. 57-59.

What to look for —

DON'T FORGET TO CONSIDER THE DIFFERENT TEMPERAMENTS.

Students of different temperaments will "see" things differently. To some, life is just "everywhere". To others, it is all in order, or should be! See TEACHER'S GUIDE, pp. 50-55.

REALISTIC RECORD

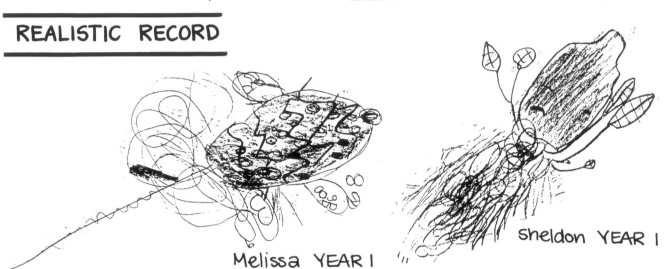

Melissa YEAR 1

Sheldon YEAR 1

Compare these drawings of the same sprouting potato. Textures in each are similar, but note the different treatments of leaves and roots. The left example is scribbly and loose. The example at right is more controlled and detailed. Does this indicate differing manipulative skills and maturity, or are different temperaments at work?! Both potatoes are the "truth" to their creators. [Note the zig-zag pattern on the left potato.]

Darrin YEAR 7

At left, is a beautiful example of sensitivity to texture. Note the "cotton-wool" treatment of the foliage compared with the clean-cut lines of the house. The CONTRAST makes the foliage softer and the wooden structure stronger. See TEACHER'S GUIDE, pp. 24, 25.

[See TEACHER'S GUIDE, pp. 24, 25.]

Martine YEAR 6

What dynamic energy is being thrown outward from this experimental piece of scraping! If the student can retain this spontaneity in her planned work, then **van Gogh can take second place** in recording the living force within a sunflower! The teacher's task is to help the student retain this confident approach and keep it in pace with the growth of maturity of ideas. It is not difficult. Just a simple, "What a marvellous sunflower that accidently turned out to be, Martine. Can you do another one just as alive as this one?"

INTELLECTUAL

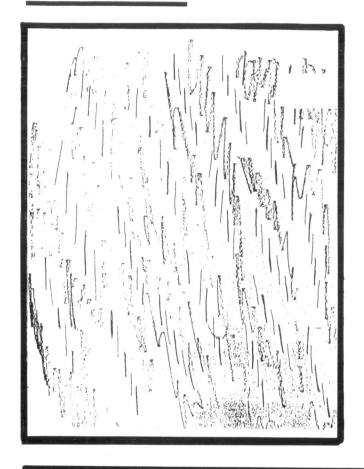

Melissa YEAR 4

At left, the student was drawing the textures of the music that was being played. So we can "read" the music as being ... fairly decisive and sharp with an "all-over" feeling of rhythm throughout; some variations occurring so that some sounds are clearcut while others are "fuzzy"; and a downward moving feeling. And so it was! See also, TEACHER'S GUIDE, p.44 and LINE, p.35. This activity is not difficult for students. But take care not to <u>suggest</u> that it is.

IMAGINATIVE

Virginia YEAR 7

The title of this work is, "What I Dream For". It shows just how textural feelings can be. The horse runs free in a transparent wash, while the child herself is "enmeshed" in turmoils that keep her from her dream. What more information could we need?

Note how the principle of SUITABILITY has been put to work in the two pieces above. See TEACHER'S GUIDE, pp. 48, 49.

Karen YEAR 10

This design started out as an exercise in combining the techniques of spattering paint from a toothbrush and using stencils. The children could select their own design ideas or follow simple directives of using only curved lines and making interesting shapes that "go in and out a lot". In the design at left, the child added the idea of superimposing the stencils over each other and varying the intensity of the stippling, both of which makes the textures scintillate.

AESTHETIC

While the child was painting this picture, from life, it was observed that "he got into the rhythm" of the textural strokes and carried them on throughout the picture because they looked "pretty good", and he was obviously enjoying the movement of the brush. In actual fact, his presentation was more "bottle-brushy" than the original!

Don YEAR 5

See TEACHER'S GUIDE, the "essential" quality approach, p.21.

PERSONAL EXPRESSION

I HATE PLANTS
Because They Come From out of the ground

Malcolm YEAR 6

Jason YEAR 6

Both these pieces of work come from the same drawing session. The students were asked to think of something they really liked or something they really disliked. They were asked to describe visually to the rest of the class what it was they liked or disliked by using SUITABLE textures as well as SUITABLE shapes. These students both obviously disliked plants — the prickly, thorny type. Both have used a scratchy texture. The lower one, with tonal CONTRAST for harsh emphasis, almost becomes pleasantly decorative, because of the child's feeling for rhythm!

Robyn YEAR 6

Leilarni YEAR 6

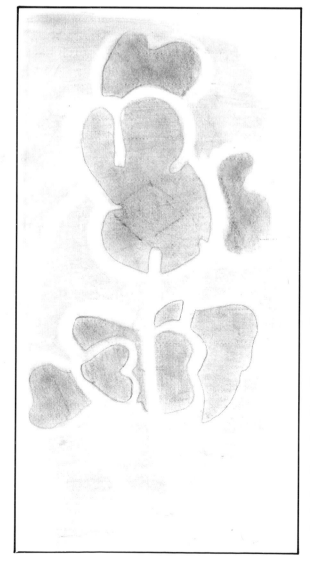

These samples came from a lesson when pencil techniques explored in TONE, Activities 20,21, were being revised in terms of texture. The most striking features of the work above are the feelings of space and movement. The soft smudging and textural blurring enhances this flowing movement. If clean hard edges had been used, the whole composition would almost "stop". The work at left, however, <u>is</u> quite "still", not only because of the vertical position of the stems, but because the edges are cleaner, more even. The masses are tex-tural but flat ~ almost like cloth. Both students have used techniques SUITABLE for their sub-jects, with textures helping to express more than the mere physical.

SOURCES FOR SUGGESTED PIECES OF MUSIC –
The following are from **ADVENTURES IN MUSIC**, a music appreciation kit prepared by Gladys and Eleanor Tipton with the Washington National Symphony, produced by Peter Dellheim, U.S.A. Most of the pieces selected for "Running on Rainbows" are well-known and readily available if the Adventures in Music kit is not obtainable.

LINE: ACTIVITY 9 – **Dance of the Reed Pipes** (from "Nutcracker Suite Op 71a)
by Peter Ilyich Tchaikovsky (Russian) . . . Grade 1, Volume 2
Twittering Machine
by Gunther Schuller (American) . . . Grade 2, Volume 2
The Swan (from "Carnival of the Animals")
by Camille Saint-Saëns (French) . . . Grade 3, Volume 2
Berceuse (from "The Firebird Suite")
by Igor Stravinsky (Russian) . . . Grade 1, Volume 1
Barcarolle (from "The Tales of Hoffman")
by Jacques Offenbach (German) . . . Grade 3, Volume 1
Symphony No. 5 in B Flat First Movement (Allegro)
by Franz Schubert (Austrian) . . . Grade 5, Volume 1

ACTIVITY 10 – **Can Can** (based on that of Offenbach's)
by Gioaccino Rossini (Italian) . . . Grade 2, Volume 1
The Changing of the Guard (from "Carmen Suite No. 2")
by Georges Bizet (French) . . . Grade 3, Volume 2

SHAPE: ACTIVITY 12 – **Aragonaise** (from "Le Cid")
by Jules Massenet (French) . . . Grade 1, Volume 1
Barcarolle (as above)
Ballet of the Sylphs (from "The Damnation of Faust")
by Hector Berlioz (French) . . . Grade 1, Volume 1
Can Can (as above)

COLOUR: ACTIVITY 12 – **Anitra's Dance** (from "Peer Gynt Suite No. 1")
by Edvard Grieg (Norwegian) . . . Grade 1, Volume 2
Ballet of the Unhatched Chicks (from "Pictures at an Exhibition")
by Modeste Moussorgsky (Russian) . . . Grade 1, Volume 1
Circus Music (from "The Red Pony", a Film Suite for Orchestra)
by Aaron Copland (American) . . . Grade 3, Volume 1
Dance of the Sugar Plum Fairy (from "Nutcracker Suite" Op 71a)
by Peter Ilyich Tchaikovsky (Russian) . . . Grade 1, Volume 2
Pantomine (from "The Comedians")
by Dmitri Kabalevsky (Russian) . . . Grade 1, Volume 1

ACTIVITY 13 — **Berceuse** (as above)
Twittering Machine (as above)
Dagger Dance (from "Natoma")
by Victor Herbert (Irish-American) . . . Grade 3, Volume 1
Can Can (as above)
From The Diary of a Fly (from "Mikrokosmos Suite for Orchestra")
by Béla Bartók (Hungarian) . . . Grade 1, Volume 2

TONE: ACTIVITY 11 – **Dagger Dance** (as above)
Ballet of the Unhatched Chicks (as above)
In the Hall of the Mountain King (from "Peer Gynt Suite No. 1")
by Edvard Grieg (Norwegian) . . . Grade 3, Volume 2
Leap Frog (from "Children's Games")
by Georges Bizet (French) . . . Grade 1, Volume 1
Walking Song (from "Acadian Songs and Dances")
by Virgil Thomson (American) . . . Grade 1, Volume 1

TEXTURE: ACTIVITY 11 – **Circus Music** (as above)
Barcarolle (as above)

The author wishes to express a warm gratitude to David Bycroft, Jodie Duthie and Sandy Rogers who have worked so hard behind the scenes to help those teachers who have kept the spirit of Running on Rainbows alive in the classroom. Also many thanks are extended to **Stresstrac** and its parent body, the **Queensland Teachers' Union Health Society** who helped make this edition a reality.

queensland teachers' union
health society